Praise for *Becoming a Goddess of Inner Poise*

"Spirituality in Chick Lit? Donna Freitas has the Inner Poise and the scholarly credentials to lead a new generation of women into to this groundbreaking conversation. Long may she flourish!"

—Grace M. Jantzen, research professor of religion, culture, and gender, University of Manchester, United Kingdom

"Turn off your TV and laptop, put down that fashion magazine, and pick up *Becoming a Goddess of Inner Poise*. Donna Freitas helps you discover that the spiritual road you're traveling isn't necessarily the religion you were born into."

—Clare Wool, producer/director, MTV

"Beneath the glittering veneer of girly gab about shoes, shagging, and shedding pounds in the genre of Chick Lit, lies the universal questions that all great literature considers: who am I? why am I here? what really matters? Donna Freitas uses her well-trained scholarly eye to ferret out and interpret the spiritual quests of young women as they seek to make sense of modern life. Her witty yet wise analysis of Bridget's and other heroines' journeys to Inner Poise provides the reader with compelling insights about the way we can engage and develop the spiritual dimension of the self. Freitas has crafted a feminist's spiritual guide grounded in the realities of Gen X culture while weaving in the wisdom of great religio-spiritual thinkers."

—Judy L. Rogers, associate professor and director of graduate studies, Miami University, Ohio

"Am completely in love with Donna Freitas's v. fabulous book. Bridget, Carrie, and their Chick Lit fans want to be smart and good, reflective and compassionate (in manner of Atticus Finch, esp. as played by Gregory Peck), but we find ourselves alienated from the spirituality dictated by most traditional religious institutions. *Becoming a Goddess of Inner Poise* shows each of us we can pursue a career, love life, and friendship without having to shove spirituality to the side. A sassy, realistic guide to spirituality for the Chick Lit generation."

—Mary Esselman, author, *You Drive Me Crazy: Love Poems for Real Life, The Hell with Love: Poems to Mend a Broken Heart,* and *Kiss Off: Poems to Set You Free*

"I confess. I see those hot pink covers with the high heels, the shopping references in the titles, and I consume. Yes, I read Chick Lit. But I never thought of it in the way Donna Freitas spells it out in *Becoming a Goddess of Inner Poise*. And now I'll never look at Chick Lit the same again. Enlightening, thoughtful, and v.v. funny, Donna Freitas celebrates the Bridget Jones in all of us."

—Julia DeVillers, author, *How My Private, Personal Journal Became a Bestseller* and *Girlwise: How to Be Confident, Capable, Cool, and In Control*

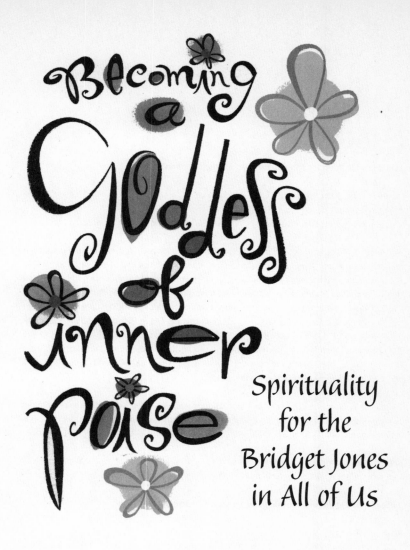

Becoming a Goddess of inner Poise

Spirituality
for the
Bridget Jones
in All of Us

Donna Freitas

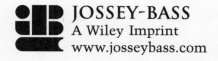

JOSSEY-BASS
A Wiley Imprint
www.josseybass.com

Published by Jossey-Bass
A Wiley Imprint
989 Market Street, San Francisco, CA 94103-1741   www.josseybass.com

Jossey-Bass books and products are available through most bookstores. To contact Jossey-Bass directly call our Customer Care Department within the U.S. at 800-956-7739, outside the U.S. at 317-572-3986, or fax 317-572-4002.

Jossey-Bass also publishes its books in a variety of electronic formats. Some content that appears in print may not be available in electronic books.

Library of Congress Cataloging-in-Publication Data

Freitas, Donna.
    Becoming a goddess of inner poise: spirituality for the Bridget Jones in all of us/
      Donna Freitas.—1st ed.
      p. cm.
    Includes bibliographical references.
    ISBN 0–7879–7628–8 (alk. paper)
      1. Single women—Religious life. 2. Catholic women—Religious life. 3. Jones,
    Bridget (Fictitious character)—Miscellanea. I. Title.
    BX2373.S55F74 2004
    248.8'43—dc22   2004014545

Printed in the United States of America
FIRST EDITION
PB Printing   10 9 8 7 6 5 4 3 2 1

Contents

To Margaret Dunn and Kylie Dixon

Where would I be without your friendship?
You are the models of Inner Poise in my life.

And to Julianna Gustafson

I knew immediately when we met how
fabulous and funny you were,
but I had no idea what a v.g. friend
you would become.

Thank you Margaret, Kylie, and Julianna,
for everything, everything, everything . . .

Acknowledgments

As Am V.V. Thankful
(in manner of ritualistic worshipfulness)

First I would like to extend my heartfelt thanks to Julianna Gustafson, editor extraordinaire at Jossey-Bass, whose enthusiasm, humor (as you are so v.v. funny), diplomacy, gift of persuasion, endless support, incredible eloquence, fashion sense, ability to withstand all manner of questions, concerns, brainstorming, ups, downs, and discussions about chocolate, shoe-shopping, weddings, my mother, etc., and whose overall Inner Poise (could you share with the rest of us, please?) has graced every page of this book. Without you, this project would still be an idea rattling around in my overactive imagination. Your "dress with wings" is v. appropriate as you are v. angelic (but in manner of fun, martini-loving angel). I must stop singing your praises somewhere (as am not v.g. singer), so I will end here by saying that I can't believe my luck to not only have the privilege of you as my editor, but to count you as a friend. Thank you, thank you, and thank you!

To *everyone* at Jossey-Bass, especially Chandrika Madhavan, Lauren Schick, Andrea Flint (whose sweetness and support during a difficult time in my life was above and beyond and so appreciated), and Jessica Egbert (for introducing me to Julianna Gustafson in the first place). You are all so amazing, supportive, funny, and wonderful, and have made this experience so much fun. I only hope that soon we can go out to celebrate on the same coast.

Thank you to Wiley for taking a chance on this book!

To the many talented, creative, extraordinary women who were instrumental in this project: Katrina Markoff (who is responsible for my Vosges, Celebration Toffee habit and has helped me to see the spirituality in my chocolate obsessions), Meg Cabot, Jennifer Baumgardner, Amy Richards, Julia DeVillers (who has helped me get "Girlwise"), Kristin Gore, Mary Esselman, Grace Jantzen (my academic mum), and Judy Rogers.

To Allen Murabayashi, you are the coolest, best photographer ever.

Like many other twenty- and thirty-something urban girls, in my numerous years as a Singleton (though will admit, am former Singleton now, but in no means am *Smug*—as prefer unSmug behavior ideally), I have been fortunate to become part of an amazing makeshift family of friends, colleagues, and mentors.

To Margaret Dunn and Kylie Dixon, my roommates from college, partners in crime, girlfriends who make life joyful and fun, I love and admire you both so, so much. I am lucky to have such fashionable, beautiful, hilarious cheerleaders. Thank you for your faith in me.

To Heather Friedman, her husband Darrin, and their beautiful little Maggie, my goddaughter (best way to become a mum I say, all the fun and bragging with none of the stress), your unconditional love always amazes me.

To Bridget Bradley Gray and husband David, for your continued presence and friendship, and also for introducing me to Bridget Jones! This book is all your fault in a way, B.

I am also endlessly grateful to Jason King, Layton Lawlor, Shelley and Todd Simmons, Lauren Murphy, Ridgeway Addison, Ellie Gompert (esp. for babysitting me while I waited for news about the book), Wendy Koenig, Molly Millwood and husband/chef Ari, Jennifer Hart Weed, Kristen Lynaugh, Kelly Novitski, Patrick Love, Adrian Hartley, Vidya Seewah, Gene Monterastelli, Sister Aideen, Roy Carlisle, Andrew Rotherham, Jonathan Gross, Kaitlin Murphy, Nancy Moser, Sarah and Jeremy Goldstein, Julie Kandall, Jeff Taylor, Scott and Sara Friesen, Julie Taiber and husband Adam, Heath Carter, Tiffany Eaves, and Sam Schlesinger.

To everyone at the Burlington Church Street Starbucks, especially Kelly Egan and Crystal Peck, whose amazing, special coffee every morning was instrumental in the writing of this book.

To my fellow colleagues and all of the wonderful students at St. Mike's, most especially my research assistant Abigail Sweetser, who was essential in the completion of this book, not to mention quite the Goddess of Inner Poise herself, and to all the cool girls (and a few guys too) in my Women's Spirituality and Feminist Theology classes, who remind me why I became a professor.

And speaking of professors, there are many wonderful teachers who have shaped my intellectual life and encouraged my quirky approach to academia, and to whom I owe much, especially Alisa Carse, Frank Ambrosio, Julia Lamm, Cynthia Crysdale, Margaret Mary Kelleher, Joseph Komanchak, and Mary Hoyt (who first taught me to write).

I would like to make special mention of Dr. Stephen Happel, who I've always thought of as my academic dad. Not only did he direct my dissertation, encourage me to write papers on Ally McBeal (how cool is that?), and get to know my friends and family, but without his guidance I would not be where I am today. He passed away earlier this year, and I miss him oh so much. He would have laughed to know I wrote this book! Perhaps he is smiling in heaven (as was always v. good candidate for high positions).

To Josh, my companion in life, who graciously puts up with my crazy writing schedule in addition to the desire to model myself after Jennifer Garner on *Alias* (a v. Inner Poised girl, one must admit), I love you so much. I am so lucky that you turned out to be my v. own Mr. Darcy. And one of the benefits of getting unSmug Married is that sometimes you are fortunate enough to inherit a fabulous and hilarious new family of in-laws. Thank you M.I.L., Pops (hee-hee), Zach, and Farrah (as you are practically family already).

To my dad, who is the best father a girl could have (as am v. much still a daddy's little girl), who I think was just as nervous as I was the day I found out I got this book. I love you so much, I am here for you always as you are for me, and I am so proud of you for all of your courage in facing the future. I need you.

And finally, in memory of my mother Concetta Lucia Freitas (otherwise known as "Miss Connie" or "Ma!" exclamation point essential here for effect), who passed away on June 4, 2004, but who I am absolutely convinced appeared to me in the form of a giant turtle crossing the road the day after she died. (My mother was obsessed with turtles and we have them all over the house.) I mean, how many times do you see giant turtles cross the road? Clearly it *had* to be my mother, reminding me of the following:

A. That she's still going to get in my way so I'd better watch out.
B. That she's found the means to permanently reside at the beach year round by reincarnating herself into an extremely cute sea creature.
C. That despite it all, she wants me to know she's still around if I need her.

Thank you Mom, for loving me all these years, and most of all, for giving me life.

Introduction

Bridget Jones: Not Your Average Spiritual Sage

THEN: Initial positive thoughts about Bridget Jones: 0 (but at the time way unconverted). Boyfriends: 0 (but had one just weeks earlier). Number of meals entirely of chocolate: many (but irrelevant as for medicinal purposes).

NOW: Epiphanies about Bridget: 1 (excellent). State of chocolate consumption: chronic (as chocolate is for celebrating as well as healing broken heart). Number of guilt-inducing Chick novels read due to Bridget's inspiration (20? 30?—at least as many as self-help books owned by Ms. Jones).

Hiding from Bridget Jones (impossible, as sees all)

~

Bridget Jones and I first crossed paths in a manner typical for many women who have met her: word of mouth. My friend had recently finished Helen Fielding's smash-hit novel and told me I absolutely must take her copy home to read it right away. She said it would make me laugh endlessly. I needed a bit of fun, and sometimes laughter is the best medicine for sadness. At the time I was nursing a disappointing breakup (v. bad), questioning my choice of career (what was a young woman in high heels and baby-Ts doing getting a Ph.D. with a bunch of monks and nuns?), and had no future boyfriend prospects in sight (as dating celibate priests not possible nor desirable option, especially in the shagging department).

Though I did take the book home, initially I resisted the advice to read it. I knew about *Bridget Jones's Diary* from various media reporting the adoration for Bridget erupting across Britain and then hopping the pond to the United States. Yet I felt like reporter Jessica Reaves from *Time*.com who, after caving and buying a copy despite her feminist leanings, committed to hiding it "safely behind Germaine Greer and Naomi Wolf" on her shelves. I assumed the book was probably fluff and sounded antifeminist (as many crit-ics claim) and therefore an unbecoming read for a graduate student studying women and spirituality. So Bridget sat untouched in the darkness beneath my coffee table, in the company, I might add, of countless issues of *Vogue* and a worn-out copy of the first Harry Potter book.

Finally, after yet another day of conducting myself in manner of the v. tragic, making various trips to the kitchen for meals entirely of chocolate, interspersed with St. John's Wort tea (excellent for the mood), I decided to give Bridget a chance. Enter Ms. Jones into my life: a woman who boldly goes where many of us are, yet where most of our fore-mothers (both spiritual and familial) never intended us to be (and now never let us hear the end of it either).

Within the first few pages, I realized my friend had been right all along: Bridget Jones and I were perfect for each other, as she is for millions of other women. She is in her thirties and neither Smug Married nor with child. At various points she manages to get the boyfriend count up to one (as continuing good work). And once, with fear and trepidation, she attributes a particularly large weight gain to a possible pregnancy, as (what turns out to be a fictional) baby "growing at monstrous and unnatural rate." Overall, her list of struggles is quite extensive, reaching beyond questions about Smug Married life and motherhood to include reflections on body image, family, sex, friends, career, feminism, and the spiritual life. Hurrah! I realized, in manner of the v. humorous, that instead of being a lonely, tragic spinster, I was boldly participating in the creation of an international community of Bridget-like women, resisting Smug Marriage and the annoying biological ticking of clocks, while laughing all the way to the bars for martinis.

Bridget Jones Becomes a Mum (without the literal having-to-give-birth part)

~

As it happens, *Bridget Jones's Diary* turned out to be just the beginning of what has become a hilarious journey into the lives of fictional women I can't help but love. Not long after finishing both the *Diary* and *Bridget Jones: The Edge of Reason,* I embarked on an indulgent and slightly clandestine foray into what is now a long list of novels by twenty- and thirty-something women. Not to mention the fact that I began searching bookstores for other Jane Austen knockoffs, complete with the requisite Darcy-esque hero (as one can never tire of Miss Bennett and Mr. Darcy, be they the originals or more contemporary versions). Melissa Nathan's *Pride, Prejudice, and Jasmine Field* is my personal favorite in this category, though it falls second to Bridget (of course).

The more I read, the more I became completely hooked on what the publishing industry has crowned "Chick Lit." Chick Lit is a genre of fiction that journalist Heather Cabot describes as featuring "everyday women in their 20s and 30s navigating their generation's challenges of balancing demanding careers with personal relationships"—a genre that has sparked its own imprint (Red Dress Ink) and that considers Ms. Jones its matriarch (see, Bridget Jones is inspirational already!). Since my addiction began, I have gleefully tackled stories like that of Becky Bloomwood (*Confessions of a Shopaholic*), Andrea Sachs (*The Devil Wears Prada*), and Cannie Shapiro (*Good in Bed*)—protagonists in whom I see at least a little of myself (and sometimes more than a little) and that of my girlfriends as well. Authors Jennifer Weiner, Lauren Weisberger, and Sophie Kinsella, among others, have created funny, romance-, career-, and weight-

> *Bridget struggles to attain what she calls Inner Poise throughout both her diaries—a kind of enlightenment fitting for the lives of today's twenty- and thirty-something women.*

obsessed Singletons of their own in manner similar to Helen Fielding's Bridget (excellent, as can't get enough of these funny females and v. important to satisfy cravings).

But *oh the guilt* I have felt as I dived into the adventures of these neurotic-seeming yet wonderfully funny heroines (note: though fallen Catholic, am still v. prone to guilt). As a budding scholar of spirituality (am becoming a flower), I thought that rather than reading about Becky Bloomwood's inability to resist a stylish pair of shoes, despite her ever-growing mountain of debt, I should be focusing my attentions on more "respectable" texts of the spiritual persuasion, like Teresa of Avila's *The Interior Castle* or the Bhagavad-Gita. I worried that in lieu of reading the Bible I was spending valuable research hours mooning over whether Bridget and Mark Darcy would finally get to shag each other (as romantic anticipation is always delicious). I supposed my admiration of selfless Mother Teresa should be greater than my respect for Melissa Fuller's (*Boy Next Door*) ability to be a model Christian-like neighbor *while at the same time* landing herself a sexy, good-hearted man to sleep with at night. After all, I had gotten myself into the business of studying about spirituality and women, not Chick Lit novels, and obsessing about the romantic lives of fictional characters did not seem fitting for a feminist scholar (all v. confusing I have to say).

Becoming Spiritual Epiphanied About Chicks (v.v. good, as relieves guilt)

~

Well, several re-reads later of *Bridget Jones's Diary* and following Renée Zellweger's impressive turn at channeling our beloved heroine onto the silver screen, I had my own spiritual epiphany about Bridget and her fellow Chick Lit heroines. I began to think of Bridget Jones and the other characters I secretly loved as model spiritual figures for my generation of women—as alternative goddesses of a sort (Yessss!). Bridget struggles to attain what she calls Inner Poise throughout both her diaries—what I now see as a kind of enlightenment fitting for the lives of today's twenty- and thirty-something women (those of us nourished on *Ally McBeal,* then *Sex and the City,* and now *Good in Bed* on the small screen). For Bridget, Inner Poise is both an ethical way of being and a spiritual goal. Achieving Inner Poise will not make her an all-powerful, all-knowing Diva (in manner of *The Devil Wears Prada*'s icy, inhuman tyrant Miranda Priestly) but rather a compassionate goddess-figure, who knows what's good for herself and likewise realizes that what's good for her own happiness includes loving and being loved by others (on many levels, ahem). By looking at Bridget's character, we learn that achieving Inner Poise is not about steeling ourselves against the world as if we are almighty, distant god-figures but about discovering the messier side of the divine: a god/dess that feels, cares, yearns, grieves, and knows when life calls for laughter (v. important qualities)—one who is alive in all of us.

At first glance, claims about Chick heroines as Inner-Poised goddess-figures may sound far-fetched, especially given that Cannie Shapiro, Becky Bloomwood, and Bridget Jones are all fictional characters whose inner dialogue includes a good deal of swearing and self-doubt, intermingled with ruminations about needing a good shag. They are not exactly saints, I know. Yet looking to the saints or the Dalai Lama as spiritual models is a walk in the park. While that is all fine and good for some people (the saintly life, I mean), the average woman today will never be a saint (at least in the official sense). We are not women who claim, like the medieval women mystics, to have special experiences or knowledge of the divine or that we've met Jesus in a moment of ecstatic union (though we may indeed claim that we've met other, less divine men in moments of ecstatic union). We are part of that generation stuck in the in-between stage, like when you're trying to let your hairstyle grow out but it's in a place where it never quite looks right. We are the women who reap the opportunities that our mothers wanted but didn't have—who now, because of all this choice, are kind of the odd women out as far as religion goes (and in terms of our futures as the next Mother Teresa). We have all this feminist consciousness but still count our calories; we have sexual freedom without the guilt (sometimes), and we can pursue careers in addition to having babies if we want. All this womanly choice makes the saintly life a long shot for most of us, makes religion impossible for some of us, or just a once-a-week ritual venture for the rest of us.

The value of seeking the divine in the Bridgets of Chick Lit and the Carries of Chick TV is that, once we find it there, it is only a short path to seeing it in ourselves. Like Bridget, who craves Inner Poise and spiritual epiphany, we (her readers) crave a meaningful, fulfilling life and a place to fit our souls neatly and snugly in the same way we crave our comfy sheets and yummy duvets, our next issue of *Vogue,* and a night out with the girls. Most of us *are* seeking something like

Inner Poise in our lives, though we may not have labeled it in the same way as Bridget. While the spiritual distance between Mother Teresa and most of us is so great she's almost too far away to imagine, I often feel like Bridget is sitting directly across the breakfast table. Likewise, while Mother Teresa's spiritual relevance shines as brightly as the sun to just about everyone, Bridget's rather merely twinkles only here and there, sometimes hidden by stormy weather. Like many of us, she is a spiritual underdog of sorts. In the Bridget Joneses and Carrie Bradshaws of our collective imagination, we may have to look a little harder to find the divine lurking. These women may never be saints, but neither will most of us. I find it more productive to start with the real than with the ideal (all v.g., as important to make connections between spiritual leanings *and* extensive shoe collection, not to mention dating history). Besides, if the likes of Britney Spears and Madonna can claim themselves Kabbalists in Jewish mystic fashion, then surely we can give heroines as popular as Bridget a chance to say something about spirituality for the benefit of the millions of women who love them.

How This Book Works (and why it won't require you to wear a nun's habit)

~

Becoming a Goddess of Inner Poise offers Bridget as a kind of bridge between traditional and academic conversations about spirituality and those of us who are fans of the characters and authors of Chick Lit (and Chick TV, too). In the chapters that follow, I search for spiritual wisdom in Bridget Jones *instead of* Mother Teresa, in Cannie Shapiro *in lieu of* a Buddhist nun, in Becky Bloomwood *rather than* medieval mystic Julian of Norwich. And though heroines other than Bridget of the Chick persuasion may not *explicitly* seek Inner Poise, by viewing their journeys in light of Bridget's, we can begin to see how Inner Poise indeed is alive in their stories and in the similar struggles they face in relationships, work, and body image, among other things. By doing this, I believe we can encounter a different spiritual model of sorts— one that is relevant to the

All this womanly choice makes the saintly life a long shot for most of us.

unique issues women face today and the new paths before us (that are different from those of our mothers)—one that also fits within the current trends in scholarship about women and spirituality. Seeking spiritual enlightenment through story has quite a distinguished history (which I will explain further in Chapter One), not to mention that all religions have their sacred myths, though, indeed of a rather different sort than Chick Lit (as you might imagine).

Now that I've introduced you to Bridget Jones as the new feminine model for the spiritual sage, it's time for us to begin exploring Inner Poise and goddess-hood through the various adventures of our favorite fictional protagonists. This book is organized thematically into eleven chapters, each representing an important "struggle" on Bridget's spiritual journey in particular but also interweaving the stories of fellow Chick heroines where relevant. The beginning sections of every chapter introduce a particular struggle important to women's spirituality through Bridget's diary writings and adventures, with an occasional personal anecdote thrown in. The middle sections explore the role of this struggle in light of spiritual autobiography and feminist spirituality, and often draw wisdom from Christian, Jewish, Islamic, and Buddhist spirituality as well. Finally, each chapter concludes by discussing how we can view the struggle of Chick women in the context of our own spiritual journeys. Feel free to enter the dialogue at whichever chapter is most relevant to your particular path, since you do not have to read them in order of first to last. Each chapter stands on its own (v. convenient).

Last bit of advice to readers (I promise): By way of Chick Lit, this book raises more questions about the spiritual themes it explores than it purports to solve. An institutionalized religion of Chicks is not my intended result (though what an interesting religion it might be!). The motivation to write what follows began with one simple question: What does it mean that so many of us today find ourselves expressed in women like Bridget, so much so that we end up re-reading—almost literally gobbling up—her adventures and those of others as if they were candy (preferably of the Vosges Haute Chocolate variety, if you are me)? That's a big question to ask, and determining a response fit for all women is not an easy task; I can't pretend to have all the answers. Rather, in *Becoming a Goddess of Inner Poise* I hope to provide you, the reader, with a new framework in which to reflect on your own spiritual journey. If you are reading this now, you have probably asked similar questions about spirituality and perhaps even sought answers in manner of the

v. Bridget: through the mountains of self-help books offered to women like us today. But in going forward from here, take off your cute shoes, pour yourself a glass of wine (as alcohol units v. helpful when reading), and stop worrying so much about answers (as can be v. stressful); just let yourself "be" with the questions (ooooh! sounds v. Zen doesn't it?). Questions often lead us to more interesting places anyway.

Becoming a Goddess of inner Poise

1

The Confessions of a (Neurotic) Diary-Keeper

Why Telling Our Stories Is a Spiritual Act

*Number of sacred stories today for women by women: expo-
nentially improving (v.g.). Number of "official" sacred stories
by women with whom I identify: as yet undetermined (as have
no plans to cloister myself in monastery). Number of "unoffi-
cial" spiritual narratives à la Chick Lit: multiplying by the day
(v. encouraging).*

Making Lists, Journaling,
and Other Spiritual Activities

~

"You mean that writing in a journal has something to do with
spirituality?" a thirty-something Singleton friend asks me over
coffee one day.

"Actually, yes." I respond. "The spiritual autobiography has a long history, beginning with St. Augustine's *Confessions,* and there are about a million scholars claiming that
a woman 'telling her story' is a spiritual act. Feminists in spirituality have been saying this for years now."

"Really?" she asks again, seeking confirmation.

"Really."

"So my keeping a diary *in manner of Bridget Jones* may in fact contribute to personal spiritual growth and development of Inner Poise in real life?"

"Yes."

"Wow. I've never heard that before. All this time I've been making lists and recording life, thinking it's probably just silliness, and now I find out that for years I have been embarking on a spiritual journey without even knowing it. This is all quite exciting."

"Indeed."

"What about premarital shagging? Does this also hold spiritual promise?" she presses, hopefully.

"Well . . . that's a conversation for another day."

Why All the Journaling Anyway?
~

Bridget Jones leaves nothing to the imagination in her daily diary ruminations, which range from worrying about which pair of underwear is best for a particular event (like potentially shagging her boss) to cataloging the list of self-help books she happens to be reading. She treats us to play-by-play accounts of her feelings and experiences, lists of New Year's "Wills and Will Nots," and, of course, her trademark report of calories consumed, cigarettes smoked, and alcohol units imbibed at the beginning of each diary entry. Occasionally, she even indulges us with information about the number of times she's shagged in twenty-four hours or else expressed her frustrated recollections of minutes/hours/days spent since she last got someone into bed (as Bridget is a v. meticulous record-keeper on certain issues).

Diary-keeping as a means to self-expression and improvement are high on the list of all the heroines of Chick Lit. Bridget may have been the first Chick to do it (as we know, she is the mum of all Chicks), but everyone else seemed to follow suit with wild abandon. The journaling style that gave Bridget life not only resonated with the women who devotedly read her month-to-month adventures but it launched a major trend among young women authors. They often tell the stories of their female protagonists "confession style"—in manner of Sophie Kinsella's *Shopaholic* series that stars the fashion-focused Becky Bloomwood. Meg Cabot in *Boy Meets Girl* also uses diary entries for some of her character Kate Mackenzie's juiciest moments as she chronicles her exciting dating life with a certain American barrister named Mitchell. Cabot's teenager heroine from *The Princess Diaries,* Mia Thermopolis, is never away long from her own journal either, especially when she is sitting in math class (best time for it, I might add).

In addition to diary-writing, list-making (from the v. personal to the rather banal) is also a popular literary device among Chick authors. Allison Pearson, Sophie Kinsella (esp. in *Can You Keep a Secret?*), and Helen Fielding, among others, all use lists as a way to illuminate the current state of mind, quandary, or epiphany of their heroines. Character Kate Reddy's "Must Remember" lists from *I Don't Know How She Does It* often appear at the end of a chapter and include everything from the incredibly funny ("see brill new film—Magic Tiger, Puffing Dragon?" and "get Jesus an exercise

ball," (Jesus being the name of daughter Emily's hamster) to
the rather poignant ("My mother saying my name, Kissing a
child's cold cheeks"). And, of course, Bridget Jones makes all
manner of lists throughout both diaries, including what she
has learned from many hours of reflection while imprisoned
in Thailand (note to self: prison time can be v. productive and
epiphany-oriented).

My guess is that all this journaling, diary-scribbling,
and list-making is one of the reasons we are drawn to these
novels, since this style of writing is familiar in our own lives.

> *It is when a woman finds herself, her life, suddenly spoken by a story—that's what gives it a sacred dimension, regardless of whether it is an adventure, a romance, or a comedy.*

I have friends who for
years have lovingly
kept a diary and, when
finished with one, con-
sider going out to pur-
chase another an act
of sacred importance.
Beginning a new jour-
nal can be a heavily
symbolic experience,
as we see in the first
Bridget movie when Mark Darcy buys her a new diary, hoping that the beginning of their relationship will be a new
chapter (literally) in her daily reflections (v. sweet of Darcy,
must admit). We keep lists of books we hope to read, movies
we want to rent, quotations we've heard and want to remember for always. We invest all of our hopes, dreams, and
frustrations on everything from scraps of paper we gather in
a folder to beautifully bound sketchbooks and travel journals.

Many of us feel the need to put pen to paper or fingers to keyboard as we try to stencil out our lives and what is meaningful to us. For some reason we feel the need to tell our stories, not just in conversation but in a form that we can go back to later or that perhaps will allow us to share ourselves, our memories, and experiences to another loved one someday. (Or to later publish a tell-all memoir of our sordid pasts, like in *The Kiss* by Kathryn Harrison. Though most likely our journaling is not for this particular reason. But, then again, you never know . . .)

A Woman Needs a Story (a sacred one)
~

Nobody knows better than women that history has been written by the conquerors, and those people have usually turned out to be of the white male species (perhaps of the boss, Daniel Cleaver variety). As far as sacred stories go, women have never had the best shot at starring as the heroine who saves all. Though sacred texts have shaped civilizations, it is rare that we hear from women in revelation and even rarer that feminine language is used in a positive light or to symbolize the divine. We instead inherit stories like that of Eve in Genesis, who brings future doom and death on all of humanity by disobeying YHWH (oops) and who elicits quite the moving reply from Him in response to this betrayal: "I will greatly increase your pains in childbearing; with pain you will give birth to children. Your desire will be for your husband and he will rule over you" (excellent). Sacred texts tend to express that women should be silent, submissive (and punished if they act otherwise), and not fit to represent God (as we are weak, irrational, empty vessels, and God is usually portrayed as the exact opposite).

The problem here is that, aside from rare exceptions (like medieval Christian mystic Hildegard of Bingen) and ancient goddess-culture (which contemporary scholars are working hard to retrieve), until recently women have almost never been allowed to voice their stories, especially with regard to the sacred. We have rarely been given permission to "speak" about spirituality and the divine from our perspective and life experiences, at least within the boundaries of traditional, organized religion. There has been a lack of space for the feminine in conversations about the sacred. For the majority of history, women have been forced to sit in silence, rarely endeavoring to chronicle their life journeys. As a result, centuries of spiritual wisdom and women's experience have been lost to us and future generations.

In response to the silencing of the feminine within traditional religion, scholar Carol Christ (pronounced with a short "i" by the way, and *not* in manner of the divine man himself) began claiming in the 1970s that the dearth of sacred stories that celebrate women across the world's religions has had an enormously negative impact on a woman's sense of self. Without appropriate feminine sacred examples to guide our self-development, Christ worries that we are left either repeating our mothers' lives or becoming only what men want us to be (while, of course, men try to become God). In other words, we are lacking in healthy models for our identity and self-esteem. Christ went so far as to say that if a woman is *unable* to locate herself in a positive light within sacred texts that this *stunts her growth* (and not just on a spiritual level). As men continue to try and achieve the divine-like qualities they have long attributed to God (power, knowledge, and so on), women have been left without a divinity according to our gender and to whose qualities we can aspire.

To address this problem, Christ called for "a new literature for women" that would provide alternative models for a woman's life—a life grounded in what Christ calls "spiritual quest." Spiritual quest as a chronicle of one's inner journey of self not only has a long and distinguished history within religion but also understands personal storytelling as a spiritual act. The original "spiritual autobiography" is often credited to St. Augustine, who, in his *Confessions,* tells in a deeply serious yet almost Bridget-like fashion of every failure, doubt, worry, sexual escapade, and spiritual mishap he ever experienced. Although St. Augustine may have been the first, it was not long before many other spiritual confessors followed his example. In light of this genre of autobiography, Christ began arguing that we (women) need sacred stories of our own, as these "stories reveal the powers that provide orientation in people's lives." If the only available stories of spiritual quest are those written by men (like good old Augustine), then our journeys and senses of self will never be of our own making, and seeing our lives as fertile spiritual ground will remain relatively impossible (v. bad).

Chick Lit as Sacred Text (What?!)

~

But do not despair! Though a woman voicing her life story was rare in the past, today writing by women about spirituality and the sacred is becoming more available and takes on myriad forms (it's about time). For example, Kathleen Norris, in her best-selling book *The Cloister Walk,* tells readers how the structured religious life of a monastery plays a role in her personal search for the divine. Twenty-something Lauren F. Winner tells the story of her journey from Judaism to Evangelical Christianity in *Girl Meets God*. Muslim Azir Nafisi, in *Reading Lolita in Tehran,* creatively writes her memoir of life as a woman in Iran through reflections on reading banned books. In the extraordinarily popular novel *The Red Tent,* Jewish author Anita Diamant imagines the life of Dinah, daughter of Jacob and sister of the famous dreamer Joseph. Although Dinah of the Torah is a silent victim, in *The Red Tent* Diamant brings to life what Dinah's spiritual journey might have looked like if she had been given a voice thousands of years ago. *And suddenly today* we encounter what I regard as a different sort of sacred story: the burgeoning Chick Lit genre, built in towers of pink-, yellow-, and blue-covered books that tell humorous tales of love, marriage, shoe-shopping, and credit card debt. At first glance, these stories may not seem at all like any of the examples of women's spiritual quest that I have listed. Yet just because these books look a little pink on the outside and are not written in manner of *Girl Meets God* does not make them irrelevant to how we ground our spiritual lives as women. We just have a bit of a challenge ahead in exploring how Chick Lit fits in relation to what has become the more typical means of expressing the spiritual lives of women.

The million-dollar question for us becomes, of course, how does Chick Lit stand up spiritually to the likes of *Showings,* by Julian of Norwich—nun extraordinaire from the four-

teenth century (as Julian was not doing a lot of shagging, nor
hitting the bottle, except perhaps at Church and then in v.
limited quantities, I assume)? Can we consider the non-theistic-
centered reflections by Chick heroines of a similar spiritual
significance to those of Kathleen Norris? Can the likes of
Bridget Jones's Diary and
Confessions of a Shopaholic
prove to be sacred stories,
when the closest their characters get to prayer is
through exclaiming, "Oh
God," uttered in frustration
over men or on receipt of
another letter from a debt
collector? And where exactly is the spiritual in a woman like Bridget, whose most

> Bridget articulates the identity struggles of women everywhere in manner of the v. funny, helping her audience face ambiguity with a grin rather than as if we are tragic spinsters.

explicit desire for divine status is expressed in her comment,
"Wish had not been born but immaculately burst into being in
similar, though not identical, manner to Jesus, then would not
have had to have birthday"? Or whose definition of *miracle* is
that "sex prove[s] indeed to be the best form of exercise"?

The fact that Bridget's journey does *not* pivot on religion, at least in a traditional sense, is not exactly shocking
news to her readers. Helen Fielding is not telling Bridget's
story in light of how she found God or as a way to speak
about what it means for her to be a Christian or a Jew. Though
Bridget displays an interest in spirituality, the religious life
is not her central object or goal. And though we, her readers,
may also crave spiritual wisdom, my guess is that few of us

make room for nightly readings of the Bible, the Torah, or the Bhagavad Gita in our schedules. Our encounters with religion are probably more on the level of going to services around holidays or weddings when parental units require, or in reading self-help Zen books. Although in *Cloister Walk,* Kathleen Norris searches for spiritual fulfillment through the experience of monastic life, hiding ourselves away in a monastery, interesting-sounding though it may be, is probably not high on our list of priorities. Much like us, the fictional heroines invented by Fielding, Kinsella, Weiner, and others are worldly girls, not about to take a retreat from life. Instead, these are women who remain *where they are,* looking for answers. The women of Chick Lit embark on quests that are more suitable for those "spiritual but not religious" girls who are everywhere today, or for the woman who still goes to church or temple now and again but whose life doesn't necessarily line up perfectly with the ideals of the religion she's inherited.

Aside from the fact that none of our femme fatales are nuns-turned-spiritual-sages, there is no doubt that protagonists like Bridget Jones and Kate Reddy treat us to thorough examinations of life, to *personal quests* of a sort that struggle with life's biggest themes (v.g. start). This self-examination gives their stories a solid foundation on which to begin considering whether they are indeed of a sacred caliber. Looking at their adventures as examples of "spiritual quest" in the way that Christ describes is just a decidedly different endeavor from reviewing the explicitly God-centered journeys of Catholic Worker founder Dorothy Day (*The Long Loneliness*) or Lauren F. Winner's *Girl Meets God* memoir. We will just have to read between the lines a bit to discover how the spiritual life presents itself in the stories of these fictional women.

The Telling and the Hearing (I can hear! I can hear! Have v. spiritual ears!)

~

Happily, Carol Christ has an answer for us on the God-focus–religion-centered issue in reference to spiritual quest (she seems v. all-knowing). According to Christ, a sacred story need not *always* orient a person to a particular divinity or structured religious lifestyle or practice (thank the Goddess, as cloistering self not high up on my to-do list—see, am v. prayerful). It is when a woman finds herself, her life, suddenly *spoken* by a story—that's what gives it a sacred dimension, regardless of whether it is an adventure, a romance, or a comedy (note: my interpretation here). "What is common to all [sacred] stories is not their genre but their function in providing orientation to life's flow. Indeed the same story may be sacred to one person and not another" (thank you, Dr. Christ). Thus adventure stories, romances, and humorous tales are all valid sources for the sacred. Imperative within spiritual quest, though, is that it include the struggle to understand life's biggest questions; it is through encountering new examples of struggle, "in fiction, poetry and other literary forms [that] are key sources for discovering the shape of women's spiritual quest." (All excellent news so far.)

For Christ, ultimately there are two major qualities that determine a woman's story as sacred: first, the *telling* and second, the *hearing*. For Christ, it is within us to determine the spiritual significance of a story, through "the importance given to the story by teller or hearer." The "telling" part in Bridget's and other Chick heroines is obvious (with the help of their authors, of course): they vividly and courageously write themselves into existence in all their glories and embarrassments, and never without laughter. Ironically, some of the very elements that inspire the media to criticize women like Bridget as self-absorbed, highly neurotic, prone to despair, extreme in nature, and pathetically self-deprecating (kind of like St. Augustine) are the same qualities that, I would argue, give her story a spiritual dimension. For example, what some critics charge as "self-absorption," a mystic might see as a journey inward, framed by a search for meaning and purpose. Rather than neurosis, we can say that Bridget achieves a heightened, almost mystical sense of self-awareness: a state that includes acknowledgment of her limitations (i.e. human finitude), the need for forgiveness of self and from others, as well as her capacity for visions (i.e. positive thinking), even during the depths of despair. And speaking of despair, rather than characterize Bridget's woes as pathetic, there is nary a mystic who at some point does not experience "a dark night of the soul" or two, in St. John of the Cross fashion. As mysticism scholar Evelyn Underhill notes, "The material for an intenser [more mystical] life, a wider, sharper consciousness, a more profound understanding of our own existence, lies at our gates." But to get at this "material" requires a willingness, like that of Bridget, to embark on a sometimes harrowing journey inward to the depths of our souls to see what we find (which may include more alcohol units and calories consumed in one day than we want to admit).

So the telling part is settled: the stories of twenty- and thirty-something women are certainly available to us, and in large quantities. The "hearing" part that confirms their spiritual status is the part that is up to us, their audience. Like men who have identified, written, and claimed sacred stories (the Torah, New Testament, Qu'ran) for centuries now, affirming these stories for everyone as *the* sacred ground of entire cultures (without giving anyone a choice in the matter), women today have the power to do the same: to choose our own sacred stories. The best-selling status in both Britain and the United States of *Bridget Jones's Diary, Good in Bed,* and *Confessions of a Shopaholic* and the "ritualistic" reading of these stories in countless women's book clubs, not to mention discussion of these women over lunch and coffee, indicates quite loudly that these authors and their fictional heroines *are* indeed being heard. London's *Evening Standard* actually went so far as to describe Bridget as "no mere fictional character, she's the Spirit of the Age." (Hurrah!) Oprah (who is practically a bona fide spiritual sage herself) has called *I Don't Know How She Does It* the "national anthem" for working moms everywhere (and we all know what it means when Oprah says something: it is heard by all women). If the power is truly within us to decide whether, where, and how a story has something spiritually valuable to say, then it looks like we are already making excellent progress in the hearing and affirming department and on many different levels (excellent).

We Are All Protagonists
(and this calls for a loud hurrah!)

~

We hear, we hear! And this is exactly what makes the Chick Lit version of spiritual quest significant, unique, and appealing to so many women: it's the questions and issues these stories raise for us and the fact that they do not pepper us with absolute answers that makes us love them so much. The

We should celebrate Chick Lit as a pioneer genre for our generation; we are exploring a new kind of sacred story—one that fits us in manner of a well-cut dress and not in manner of a habit.

genre of spiritual autobiography has generally been filled with what a Christian might call eschatological longing—eschatology having to do with an endpoint or future resolution. We are used to judging a person's spiritual journey by how it's resolved

through evidence of a kind of turning point or epiphany that changes everything. Yet unlike traditional accounts of spiritual journeys that begin with struggle and the writer's spiritual concerns but end with some form of resolution, at the end of stories like those of Bridget and *Shopaholic*'s Becky Bloomwood, we find these women still struggling and inquiring; their journeys lack a clear endpoint. And like the characters of Chick Lit, emerging generations of women don't have all the answers to life's happiness. Why would we? We are in uncharted territory. The "right" answers or resolutions to our struggles won't necessarily arrive in a single package, meant for everyone. (But perhaps will instead arrive in multiple, beautifully wrapped boxes from places like Tiffany's and Barney's.) There are many possible paths we might take, not all of which will lead to ultimate resolutions, most of which will only lead to temporary resolution and eventual further struggle.

There is a refreshing authenticity to these heroines' journeys. Characters like Bridget don't pretend to *have* all the answers for us; Bridget as a "goddess" or sacred figure is *not* sacred perfection. Her readers get to watch her experiments, her successes and failures, her instances of renewal and transformation, as well as regression, as we experience similar situations in our own lives. Bridget articulates the identity struggles of women everywhere in manner of the v. funny, helping her audience face ambiguity with a grin rather than as if we are tragic spinsters. Seeing glimpses of the goddess in Bridget will empower us—the millions of women who find ourselves spoken in Bridget's story—to see dimensions of the sacred in our own lives by way of the similar struggles we face and perhaps confess them in manner of Ms. Jones as well.

And confess we must, *loudly* and in all our messy uncertainty! Traditional religious perspectives have mistakenly left us with the notion that there *should* be a be-all-end-all answer to life's questions, leaving many women today feeling guilty about what, on the surface, look like lives in perpetual limbo—lives whose reality we feel should be shut away in the dark. After all, who wants to tout a story as sacred if, according to traditional spiritual standards, on paper

it seems like a sacred *failure*? As women, we have been
schooled that when it comes to the sacred, we'd best remain
silent—a lack of voice that has sparked Christian and Jewish
women to try and actually "read the silences" of women in
sacred texts to discover where the sacred feminine has been
hiding in these traditions, searching for something positive in
which we can find our sacred selves.

Yet lucky for us, unlike in the Torah or the Gospels
where it is rare to find a woman actually speaking, in Chick
Lit silence is not an issue. Our heroines are speaking loud
and clear about what it's like to be twenty-something, thirty-
something, and female. As their audience, we need to take
their audacious turns inward to remind ourselves that opening up to struggle and questioning is itself a spiritual act. We
come from a generation who has not been taught to name
this type of "recurring" struggle in spiritual terms. We are less
explicit about spirituality than generations before us and
therefore not quite as adept at naming or labeling significant
moments on our spiritual journeys in manner of men and
women like St. Augustine and Catherine of Siena in times
long past. But let's not allow the fact that our spiritual journeys look different to convince us *not* to claim them as sacred or blind us to the spiritual value of our paths. Instead,
we should celebrate Chick Lit as a pioneer genre for our generation; we are exploring a *new* kind of sacred story—one
that fits us in manner of a well-cut dress and *not* in manner
of a habit (as in nun's habit, and thank God; see—am always
thanking God—am really good Catholic girl at heart, despite
mother's arguments to the contrary).

As we begin to celebrate Chick Lit as a sacred genre for women, this should help us do the same with our own stories, journals, lists, and confessions: to read between the lines to find the spiritual dimensions that have set, perhaps mostly hidden even from ourselves, now drawing them out into the open. Like Helen Fielding, Meg Cabot, and Jennifer Weiner, who have poured life into these characters and stories, it is important for us to tell our own sacred versions of life. Women today, whether we are writing novels or private journals, are engaged in a sacred kind of myth-making, just as men have been doing for millennia now. We are taking over this process for our gender, our generation, and in our own voice, since the myth that Eve provides may not tell the whole story, or her story may be decidedly different altogether from our own. Scholar Ada María Isasi-Díaz, like Christ, insists that telling our personal stories is foundational to spirituality and advises that we must all become "protagonists" of a sort for spiritual growth to become possible. All we need now is to embrace the Inner Poise of the heroine inside each of us, letting her confess her own version of spiritual story, however quirky it turns out to be, since in the end we can all be protagonists in a spiritual quest of sorts, if we allow ourselves to be. (A loud hurrah is in order here and perhaps a chocolate martini to wash it down, as must not allow all this confessing to make us hoarse.)

2

Real Feminists Don't Wear Pink—or Do They?

Making Spirituality Fit for Chicks (in Kitten Heels)

Declaring oneself feminist (possibly v. bad)—privately ranting on in manner of angry feminist (excellent, especially when ranting includes fizzy bottles of alcohol units). Number of stereotypical man-despising feminist friends: 1 (v.g. for emergency situations resulting from interactions with emotionally unenlightened male species).

Did Somebody Say Feminist? Ssshh!

~

Throughout both diaries, Bridget is rather schizophrenic about feminism, to say the least (though only figuratively, as psychosis is unbecoming to women with Inner Poise). In one moment Bridget and Jude are shushing their friend Sharon (Shazzer) for one of her public rants about the male species, and in the next Bridget is scribbling in her diary that women must *not* appear feminist (as v. unattractive to men). Yet further on, we find Bridget exclaiming how nothing compares to a "night of drunken feminist ranting with Sharon and

Jude." Of course, as a rule any openly feminist behavior occurs in the privacy of Bridget's apartment, where said tendencies are not in danger of being noticed by others. Although behind closed doors, Bridget is not afraid to express anything at all about her body, career, motherhood, men, *and* feminism, public association with feminist raging makes her look both ways to see who's listening (as would not want to scare off potential dateable man).

Shazzer represents what our culture views as the archetypal, man-hating feminist in Bridget's diaries. Whenever we encounter her, she is usually shouting, ranting, or hoping to inspire righteous fury in her typically less angry friends. Bridget describes Shazzer in "top form" when she is exhibiting behavior that involves loud yelling, usually about men, and complimenting the male species as "stupid, smug, arrogant, manipulative, self-indulgent bastards." Not exactly subtle. At one point her growling reaches such an intense level that even police officers become frightened of her (as said officers are present due to Bridget's return from her Thai, thigh-slimming prison experience—more on this next chapter). In *The Edge of Reason,* Shazzer does relent a bit in the man-hating department, and we learn of her shockingly un-Shazzer-like conduct regarding a "special friendship" with Simon, which later reduces her to tears, albeit angry ones, when things don't go so well. But true to character and aside from this aberration, Shazzer eventually returns to her original, angry feminist form.

Getting back to our hesitatingly feminist heroine Bridget, in one scene we find her in a conversation with Mum that captures the tension that many twenty- and thirty-something women feel about feminism (the kind of tension that makes all self-proclaimed feminists cringe when confronted with it). In this particular scene, Bridget exclaims to her mother at one point, "But if you're a feminist, you shouldn't need a . . ." Finish the sentence here with the word *man* and, in doing so, imagine the faces of self-proclaimed feminist scholars everywhere wincing and cringing at said implication. In response to Bridget's comment, Mummy explains, with all seriousness, that this notion behind feminism that a woman shouldn't need a man (or anyone else for that

If we are beyond letting our mothers pick our shoe style, then we are certainly beyond letting them pick out our feminism and our spiritual lives.

matter) to make her happy is what makes feminism so *silly*. After all, as Mum says, "Anyone with an ounce of sense knows we're the superior race. The only problem is when they think they can sit around when they retire and not do any housework" (they, of course, being *men*).

If only Mummy's assurance were really true for women (people knowing about our obvious superiority, I mean), then we wouldn't need to be going about worrying so much about the whole feminist issue, right? If only it was this easy. Unfortunately for us, Mummy's dismissal of feminism as silly, in a manner typical of Bridget's mum's overall ridiculousness, does not grapple deeply enough with questions about feminism for younger generations of women. Like many of us, Bridget and her friends display a range of feelings about feminism, including intense ambivalence, celebration, and fear of association with man-hating female creatures (as hatred directed at male species is not the ideal mode of expressing self while trying to catch member of said species). Bridget's confusion, Mummy's dismissal, and Shazzer's portrayal of the ravingly mad feminist figure are all significant: they represent the wide range of experiences in our struggle to identify (or distance) ourselves with a movement orchestrated by older generations of women (our mothers) who are reluctant to let feminism evolve into something more fitting to the concerns of their daughters (us). Yet the questions at hand for us here are the following: Are Inner Poise and feminism incompatible? Or does feminism (albeit our own version) have something to offer us on our spiritual journeys and therefore something important for us to embrace?

But I Enjoy Being a Girl! (and especially wearing an abundance of pink)

~

Anxiety about and even fear of identifying ourselves as feminist in manner of Ms. Jones is a common affliction among women today. (Nervously include self here, as am guilty at various points of desire to disassociate self from unbecoming stereotypical image of ranting, feminist banshee like Shazzer. Hopefully will not now be ejected from feminist circles as result of said admission.) The vast majority of men certainly don't think feminism has anything to do with them, evidenced by the fact that on college campuses everywhere classes that fall in the "Women's/Gender Studies" category inevitably fill up with mostly female students (as the vast majority of men apparently don't know that *gender* also applies to the male species). You would think that from the women's front there would be a strong association with feminism, but most of the college-aged women I've talked with and many of my friends for that matter are reluctant to label themselves with The Word. What many of us associate with feminism seems un-attractive or irrelevant to our life concerns today (at least on the surface).

My college roommate Margaret, who was a Women's Studies minor, likes to remind me about my own outspoken resistance to feminism back in our undergraduate days—at which point, you could also find me in pony-tail with bow, waving pom-poms around and jumping up and down in cel-ebration of male testosterone-filled sporting events. (Really. I'm not making this up.) As a college cheerleader, I happily expressed, whenever pressed on the issue: "Absolutely not! I am decidedly not a feminist!" I would proclaim this in the good company of our fellow roommate Kylie, as she and I would lie on the couch, waving evil magazines like *Vogue* and *Elle* in Margaret's face with glee. Hurrah for Girlieness! My understanding of feminism back then (and sometimes still) included the following top five notions about what a feminist does and does not do:

A Feminist Does	*A Feminist Does Not*
❦ Express hatred of men	❦ Need a man
❦ Rant and rave constantly about equal rights with angry look on face	❦ Laugh and humorously acknowledge possible differences between genders

❦ Dress as if fashion doesn't matter, preferably hiding body entirely in baggy sweaters and pants, as well as wears mannish hairstyle

❦ Get caught wearing girlie pink outfits or oohing and aahing over stiletto-heeled shoes to match girlie pink outfits

❦ Decry fashion industry and waif-like model-looking creatures

❦ Read utter wickedness like *In Style, Bazaar,* and *Us Weekly*

❦ Always say what's on mind regardless of possible offending of opposite sex as probably deserves it anyway

❦ Care what anybody thinks of her as long as she advances cause of women's ultimate domination over men

(As a last-minute addition to the list, I will mention the typical disassociation made between feminism and the whole cheerleading thing, which all my male friends love to wave over my head whenever I am now discussing feminist leanings. Pun intended.)

We Are Feminists Gone Underground (but not literally as might ruin heels)

~

Then I went to graduate school (where there was no pom-pom waving at all, at least not on my part) and discovered feminism for what seemed like the first time through what some women were saying about spirituality. My initial intention was not to study feminist spirituality—or even women-and-spirituality for that matter—just plain old spirituality, period. What I discovered rather quickly, however, was that though I didn't quite feel like a feminist in manner of Betty Friedan (*The Feminine Mystique*) or Naomi Wolf (*The Beauty Myth*)—two feminists among a range of others I began to read in my classes—in fact, my life had been drastically affected by these women whom I had earlier dismissed without much thought.

Most of all, though, I liked what feminist scholars of spirituality were saying about women's voices, writings, and discussions as sacred texts and foundational to our spiritual growth. I was excited to hear these women claim that we need to imagine the divine, not just as father but as mother, sister, friend, and lover, and not only as transcendent and far away but instead right here within us and in our relationships, as much a part of the world as not. I liked how Carol Christ, Ada María Isasi-Díaz, and Dorothee Soelle, among others, described a god/dess that empowers us in lieu of punishing us, that urges us to reach out to others, challenging oppression and injustice when we encounter it. Feminists approach spirituality in a way that speaks to me differently from nonfeminist scholarship, because feminists think about the spiritual life from the particularities of women's experience. I may still hesitate over the words "I am a feminist," but my hesitation is tempered with the knowledge that feminists *are* helping me see my own life as fertile spiritual territory in ways I would not have previously imagined and in ways that the priests I grew up with and the male philosophers I have studied have *not* shown me how to do. Ever since graduate school, my association with feminism has been, well, *com-*

plicated (as am still prone to prefer calling myself a girl rather than a woman, squealing over friends' latest hookups, and drooling over hot guys at the movies—all things that still don't seem to add up well with traditional feminism).

In *Manifesta: Young Women, Feminism and the Future,* Jennifer Baumgardner and Amy Richards sort through the many issues that scare younger women like myself away from feminism, even dedicating their book to all the "buts" that come between us and feminism. Their dedication reads, "To feminists everywhere— including those of our generation who say, 'I'm not a feminist, but . . .' and others who say, 'I *am* a feminist, but . . .'" (I am one of these "but girls." Not sure that sounds becoming, but you get what I mean, hopefully.) Baumgardner and Richards recognize that the stereotypes we often associate with the feminism our generation has inherited may indeed seem outdated and even unattractive to us. Unlike most of our mothers, we've grown up wearing pants and playing sports, with many of us looking forward to a higher education, as well as a diverse array of career choices ahead of us. But what if, in addition to pants, we want to wear cute skirts? What if, after reading about "the beauty myth," we still take joy in an afternoon filled with *Elle, Vogue,* and shopping trips? What if, despite our knowledge that we are supposed to be beyond *needing* a man, our hearts

We are less concerned with reforming one tradition to fit our needs and in its place are creating quite the versatile spiritual wardrobe (as "we" are women who love to shop).

are still aflutter the afternoon before a much-anticipated date or when our latest crush brushes past us? Can one still be a feminist *and* oooh and aaah over the perfect baby-T or cute guy at the other end of the bar or the darling little baby at the next table? Can we be feminist *and* have pink as our favorite color? (As pink is new black and prim is in! Hurrah!)

The societal pendulum often swings from one extreme to the other, especially when it comes to issues like feminism (just say the word loudly in front of a group of men—"Feminism!"—and watch them start to twitch and growl). We need to be careful not to let ourselves get hit in the head in our rejection of something, without which we would not be the college-educated, career-oriented, Independent Girls that we are (not to mention that large, egg-shaped protrusions from head v. unattractive). Regardless of where we locate ourselves personally with regard to feminism, it is worth asking how, along with Bridget and friends, so many of us have ended up abandoning, at least in name, a movement that is responsible for giving us opportunities that our mothers and grandmothers only dreamed about, not to mention alternative ways of thinking about spirituality, the divine, and the religious life. Rather than disassociating ourselves with the label, I think Baumgardner and Richards are right in claiming that we need to figure out what our generation's "brand" of feminism means to us (hmmm . . . Chanel? Feminism?).

Baumgardner and Richards argue that those of us who are more likely to identify with the Girl Word rather than The Other Word indeed offer a kind of feminism that older women have overlooked. We just have yet to come together, talk about it, and flesh it out. Our version of feminism comes complete with its own political agenda about women in the workplace, sex, motherhood, and feelings of female empowerment, among other things. We are twenty- and thirty-something women who celebrate our diversity, both sexual and ethnic, watch *Sex and the City,* engage in intellectual and career pursuits, love Prada, *and* participate in politics, among other things. We play sports, date, discuss emotional deficiency in both the male and female genders, choose to have babies or not while Smug Married or not, and have lots of shags if we feel like it. We see the Girlie subversiveness in Reese Witherspoon's character Elle from *Legally Blonde* and cheer her triumphs within a profession dominated by men *and* women who underestimate the intelligence, wit, and abilities of a girl who garbs herself in lots of pink (and carries a small dog in her purse). We have all this feminist consciousness, minus the martyr complex of our mums (hurrah!). *But* our feminism is missing the organization, activism, and speaking-out part—elements that Baumgardner and Richards urge in both *Manifesta* and *Grassroots* (their latest book) that our generation needs to start discussing. (Yessss! And let's not forget that speaking out has spiritual value, not to mention that "organizing" can occur over lunch, goodies, or even a shopping trip in manner of *Sex and the City.*)

Feminist Spirituality Needs to Discover Its Inner Chick (and its Inner Poise)

~

I agree wholeheartedly with the authors of *Manifesta* that those of us who are in our late twenties and thirties (the audience of Chick Lit) have our own version of feminism and that we need to figure out what it means to us. As I read their words, I encounter a picture of feminism quite different from the more traditional version I have become used to—one that has empowered me to begin taking all the good I find in the feminist spirituality of my "mothers" to see where it might fit (and where it doesn't) in the lives of women my age. Despite our confusion and, at times, ambivalence about feminism, it is a significant topic to consider with regard to our spiritual journeys, as it does have a lot to say of value about our relationship to the divine.

As Baumgardner and Richards claim, our generation already *has* its own version of feminism in general. I believe we already have our own version of *feminist spirituality* as well—one that we need to get together and talk about, too. As we shouldn't let or even want another generation to define what feminism means to us, so we shouldn't let another generation decide for us what spirituality means to us either. That's *our task*. I am not saying we shouldn't thank our mothers for the paths they have cleared for us; we need to honor their hard work that we benefit from today. But those of us who see ourselves in the Beckys, Bridgets, and Kates of literature need to begin paying attention to what these protagonists say to us and about us, and how they express our generation's spiritual version of feminism, girlism, chickism—whatever we choose to call it. It is up to *us* to start announcing to the world how these women express new spiritual questions, paths, and experiences and what spirituality means to today's twenty- and thirty-something women. To leave this task up to our mothers would be a mistake; our style is quite different. After all, if we are beyond letting our mothers pick our shoe style, then we are certainly beyond letting them pick out our feminism and our spiritual lives. If we don't take up this task on our own, we are going to end up perpetually trying to shimmy ourselves into a set of rules for spirituality that don't quite fit (in manner of Emma from *Can You Keep a Secret?* who is continually trying to squeeze herself into a size four when she is really a size eight. Not going to happen!).

And while we are on this topic, as a young woman with a Ph.D. in spirituality, I confess that I now see a great irony, even a void, within the conversation among women scholars in my field. Recently, the hot topic of discussion about women and spirituality has revolved around an acute awareness that we need to attend to race, ethnicity, economic status, and sexual orientation in writing on spirituality, which has led to many fruitful conversations about the variety of women's experiences of the divine, organized religion, spiritual journey, and so on. In light of this critique, women scholars have begun to explore the impact of diversity and plurality on women's experiences to empower voices previously on the margins of conversation or that were formally silenced altogether with regard to the sacred. (I echo a resounding yes to all of the above endeavors, by the way.) Yet despite the attention to the diversity of women's spiritual experiences, there is an almost across-the-board *lack* of consciousness among women scholars about the relevance of *age* in women's spirituality.

I feel this gap between me and my women colleagues—many are between one and three decades older than me—all the time. I experience our differences on a number of levels: how we talk, the books we read, what we watch on television and at the movies, and especially with respect to how we look on the surface. I find myself waltzing into rooms full of scholars and wearing high-heeled, bright-pink, pointy-toed shoes with a stylish outfit to match (imagine self here as fashionista in manner of Carrie Bradshaw). Adorning myself with such things as chic shoes (symbols of materialism), reading fashion magazines that enlightened young women are supposed to reject, carrying a copy of *Bridget Jones's Diary* instead of writings by a medieval mystic, and bringing these things into the sacred boundaries of an academic discussion about spirituality helps remind me of how different I am (not to mention rather lonely) from my colleagues. The women who are supposed to be my scholarly peers are really more like my scholarly mothers—women to whom I am grateful but with whom I have trouble identifying. Among them I often feel out of place, irrelevant to what is discussed, and symbolic of everything spirituality is *not* supposed to be, especially as I totter in my favorite heels, while they wear their comfortable flats, and call myself "spiritual," while they firmly identify as Christian or Jewish.

Yet despite my feeling out of place, I am confident that my personal style as a young woman happily (though not uncritically) immersed in the world—an embracer of pop culture, a watcher of *Sex and the City,* a woman who sees herself in Bridget in body, mind, and spirit—*is* deeply spiritual terrain. It's just a deeply *unexplored* and *unarticulated* spiritual terrain, in much the same way that feminism in general for our generation is also unarticulated to a degree. All of this

felt difference regarding feminism and spirituality—the prod-
uct of growing up in a different generation—calls for our
own version of what it means to be a woman and be spiritual today. Although many of us *have* grown up in Christian
or Jewish families (some more practicing than others), where
our mother's generation has held on to tradition, somehow
we Bridget Joneses have not inherited this luxury. We may
still attend church weddings and bar/bat mitzvahs when invited, and even have them ourselves, and we may go to services on important holidays. But rather than pick up the Bible
to see how it could empower our spiritual identities the way
scholar Elisabeth Schüssler Fiorenza does, we are instead por-
ing over self-help Zen books rather than Hebrew scripture
(or happily *in addition* to Hebrew scripture). We are uncertain about where to find our spiritual centers and tend to be
more comfortable with picking and choosing from a multitude of religious teachings, not worrying ourselves so much
about sticking to a single faith. We are spiritual floaters of a
sort, and where our mothers' generation has fought hard to
change the one tradition they grew up with, we are less concerned with reforming one tradition to fit our needs and in
its place are creating quite the versatile spiritual wardrobe (as
"we" are women who love to shop).

Ultimately, it is up to *us*—the audience of Chick Lit,
those of us who find our lives, our hopes, our struggles in
these fictional women—to decide how these books are valuable and transformative on a spiritual level for our generation
in the same way that Carol Christ insists that what appears as
sacred story can vary from one person to the next. In many
ways, I think the spirituality of women changes from one

generation to the next, in the same way that women's experience can differ, depending on ethnicity, education, and tradition. Lucky for us, we have the ideas behind the feminism and feminist spirituality of our mothers' generation to provide us the foundations on which to begin our reflections and conversations.

Feminism has always been about choice—about getting to decide for ourselves which viewpoints, which opportunities, which stories, *which voices* best express who we are, where we hope to go, and who we hope to become. And feminist spirituality is no different on this issue. By reflecting on our own lives and experiences as spiritual terrain in manner of the Bridgets of Chick Lit, we can begin to see how *we* are constructing our own version of feminist spirituality (perhaps better called Chick Spirituality)—one that is relevant to a generation of women who are different from their mothers, whose endeavors to attain Inner Poise may require a variety of spiritual fittings—and a Girlie Feminine Divine that wears a lot of pink (and blue and yellow and green, but always has, of course, that perfect little black dress somewhere in the back of her closet, if the occasion arises).

3

"Oh God, Why Am I So Unattractive?"

Understanding the Body as Spiritual Temple, Not Grotesque Obstacle

Current weight: not telling. Number of Vosges chocolate units consumed while writing this chapter: 6 (v. yummy). Number of calories consumed in approximately 5 minutes: thousands (but do not count as necessary for inspiration). Number of protein units in each chocolate: 1 (excellent as am practically keeping to Atkins-like diet if not counting the sugar).

Jailtime and Liquid Chocolate as Alternative Dieting Methods

~

Like many of her female contemporaries (dare I say most, myself included), Bridget is weight-obsessed. She relentlessly counts every calorie, measures her thighs, and attempts to sweat off alcohol units and Cadbury Milktray in desperate excursions to the gym. She is convinced she would be more lovable, successful, fashionable, and sexy if she could just conform her body to a size that would allow her to fit into jeans meant for a twelve-year-old girl or, better yet, something by Marc Jacobs recently seen traveling down the runway. Thinking about Bridget in terms of body and beauty can't help but evoke images from the movie. Some of my favorites include the following: Bridget in a bunny outfit at the Tarts-and-Vicars party (which turns out to be short on Tarts and Vicars); Bridget pulling on gigantic, grandma underwear for a date with boss Daniel; Bridget running through the snow-covered London streets in a jacket and panties to find Mark Darcy. Overall with regard to Bridget's battle with her body, at the end of her first diary we learn she has lost a total of seventy-two pounds (excellent!), but then we are told that over the entire year she actually gained seventy-four (oh well—can't have everything). Bridget simply does not have the luxury of living in a Victorian-attired society in manner of Elizabeth Bennett, whose bottom remained largely hidden in flattering, empire-waist gowns that instead enhanced an ample bosom.

One of the most memorable scenes in Bridget's diaries (regarding the ever-fluctuating state of her arse) is when she makes it down to 119 pounds (hurrah!), shimmies herself into a sexy black dress, and proudly and slimly arrives at the party of her friend Jude. Bridget is ready to show off her new-and-improved bodily state yet is quickly met with a series of dismaying questions upon her arrival. "God, are you all right?" asks Jude immediately, when she sees Bridget at the door. After Bridget explains she has lost seven pounds, Jude, while staring at Bridget's "deflated cleavage," comments that "Maybe you've lost it a bit quickly off your . . . face" (which we know is code for "You've lost it all in your boobs"). Over the remaining evening, Bridget is told that she looks, among other things, drawn, tired, and flat, and she even receives a concerned, post-party phone call from Tom claiming that she looked better before. Thus Bridget's "historic and joyous day" turns into a realization that after "eighteen years of struggle, sacrifice, and endeavor," her "life's work has been a total mistake" (especially since intentions were to slim thighs not boobs). And, alas, Ms. Jones didn't learn from her prior experience, since after landing herself in a Bangkok prison (on a Thai vacation with Shazzer, no less), she rationalizes a potentially tragic jail experience into an excellent pound-losing, thigh-reducing affair.

Similar to Bridget's positive rationalization of her stint in a Thai prison, I will confess here to uttering my own secret, joyous "hurrahs!" in response to a rather unfortunate fall I had not long ago. I was left with both jaw and mouth injured in such a way that I could only consume liquids (mainly large vats of liquid chocolate) and very tiny chopped-up pieces of sashimi for approximately three months. But rather than grieve this unfortunate situation, I instead saw it as an opportunity for bodily purification in manner of self-disciplined slimming regimen! I watched (v. silently) as pounds disappeared while I sipped my miracle, exercise-free, anti-Atkins diet of chocolate soup and started fitting myself into fashionably sexy low-rider jeans, like Britney Spears (at least from waist down). A complete inability to smile or move my lips was a minor inconvenience, as it enhanced my self-image as a supermodel-like figure walking down a catwalk in a sexy pout. And, of course, at the pinnacle of my waif-like bodily state, I received many Jude- and Tom-like comments from friends registering their concern at how "thin I had become since the accident." Translation: "Wow, you look horrible, and your face is hollow in addition to being immobilized by injury" (life's work all a waste).

Bodily Obsession: Transformative or Tragic?

~

After acquiring an array of knowledge regarding the beauty myth, à la Naomi Wolf, and the problematic influence of magazines like *Vogue* and *Elle* on a woman's body image, my warning bells are set to go off at the weight-induced obsessions of Bridget and my own tendency to rationalize negative situations as slimming opportunities. The beauty myth advises us that Bridget-style calorie counting, despair over poundage gain, as well as the understanding of weight loss as our life's work, is tragic in nature. Like many women today, we grow up well aware of how cultural expectations, religious institutions, and the fashion industry (almost always orchestrated by the male species) shape our mind-set regarding our bodies, beauty, and what we wear. I know enough to cringe at cultural trends like *Rolling Stone*'s recent parade of mostly naked female pop stars on its covers, most memorably (I think, anyway) the October 2, 2003, issue with Britney baring it all from the waist up, pressed against a wall (v. porno). But I am also honest enough to get the humor in Bridget's journaling about her weight, since though I know when to cringe, I also know the realities regarding our bodies with which most of us still struggle (and when seen through Bridget are really quite funny, which is liberating in and of itself). No matter what we read about women's body and beauty images, it's difficult to shake our desire to fulfill them (though not necessarily in manner of naked appearance on magazine cover), and Bridget's obsessive calorie counting makes us laugh because so many of us obsess as much as she does.

On the topic of body image, in addition to Bridget's well-chronicled, detailed struggles with weight, thigh circumference, and daily calorie intake, Cannie Shapiro, from Jennifer Weiner's *Good in Bed,* is also a kindred spirit. And a complex one. When her ex-boyfriend very publicly announces that he considers her a "larger woman," Cannie retains a sense of humor about her body, but she is unable to maintain Bridget's optimism in her struggles with weight.

> *Why are we, like Bridget and Cannie, always trying to climb out of our own skins? . . . Will we ever learn to fully love the bodies that we are? And what does it mean on a spiritual level if we cannot?*

Cannie endeavors to take off the pounds. Although she can laugh about her situation, the damage that being overweight causes to her self-image and self-esteem is clear and painful to experience as a reader. While Bridget keeps us laughing in a way that helps us look at our own bodily struggles with great humor, Cannie elicits both laughter and tears as we empathize with her own ups and downs, triumphs and frustrations, seeing how body image can weigh us down in an emotionally scarring way.

There is no doubt that Bridget's and Cannie's inner struggles with their bodies, though unique in their own way, are central issues (and potentially obstacles) in their march toward Inner Poise. This also makes the body one of the best places to explore their characters as contemporary goddess figures; it's difficult for a woman to tell her story without reference to her experience of the body. Chick heroines' obsessions with their bodies have been decried by many in the media as sad and tragic, especially if we consider them an accurate representation of our bodily self-image. Well, we fans of Bridget know that part of why we love her is that we *do* relate and she lightens us up on the subject. Simply calling her and others sad and tragic on this particular issue misses the significance of their struggles for our purpose here.

As we think about spirituality, we need to consider the roles that body image and beauty play for us, in terms of our spiritual identity and how we think about the divine. The fact that Bridget and Cannie so honestly and humorously confess what so many of us think not only endears them to us but helps us ask some important questions. Why are we, like Bridget and Cannie, always trying to climb out of our own skins? Why are we never satisfied with what we are born with, even if we come into the world looking like the goddess-figure her boss Daniel is shagging behind Bridget's back? What is it about our willingness to endure plucking, shaving, painting, and fasting—all in the name of fashion and our drive to be beautiful and thin? Can we find the divine somewhere lurking among all of this primping and obsessing? Will we ever learn to fully love the bodies that we are? And what does it mean on a spiritual level if we cannot?

We Are But Mere Vessels
(endlessly hungry ones, it seems)

~

Women's concerns about calories, bra size, fashion sense, and thigh circumference go far deeper in history than our current exposure to wafer-thin models in magazines and, in fact, can be found rooted in religious history (bet you never thought you'd read "bra size" and "religious history" in the same sentence, but there they are). As women, we have the misfortune of inheriting a history where our bodies have traditionally and literally been seen as the property of men. In addition, a woman's capacity for reproduction (the biology-is-destiny idea) has historically determined her spiritual value (or her being devalued) in Western religion. In Christianity and Judaism, following Eve's apple-eating antics, both Adam and Eve learned to be ashamed of bodily nakedness, and Eve's punishment was to become the vessel to Adam's children, in utter pain and by command of God. Though a woman's body as a vessel for children *is* esteemed in religion, a woman's bodily capacity for childbearing has led to her association with death, since giving birth is also coupled with God's ejection of humanity from paradise and our loss of immortality (v. bizarre and unfortunate).

The traditional male-female spiritual hierarchy is as follows: women's bodies are regarded as passive in bodily development, sex, and reproduction. We can *see* a woman's body change in her development of curves, as if her body announces itself to the world. These changes *happen* to her in full view of everyone, whereas a man's bodily changes, lucky for him, remain hidden. (In other words, boobs just grow whether we like it or not.) In sex, the man is the "active" party, and the woman (supposedly) lies passively while the man "plants his seed." Then following sex we "get" pregnant, and our bodies are tied down for upwards of a couple of years if breastfeeding, emphasizing our weak bodily state. The Catholic Church goes so far as to forbid women to take precautions against getting pregnant, since they have to remain subject to "natural biological reproductive processes," as prescribed by God through scripture. This ultra-positive (am being sarcastic) view of women's bodies, of course, was written into existence by all the men in charge of things in history (including the medieval philosopher-theologian Thomas Aquinas, who is famous for some shockingly negative commentary about women as "misbegotten males" that has unfortunately influenced Christian understanding over the centuries).

All of the above have had a tremendous impact, not only on women's body images today but also in how we understand (or disassociate from) our bodies in relation to our spiritual identity and whether or not we are able to imagine the female body as divine. While for millennia we have been tied up with baby-making, men have not only gone out and ruled the world, laying the foundations for society and culture, but they have restricted images of God to masculine language, the male body, and male ideals of absolute power and perfection. Men see themselves as the *active* sex: the participants in public life, the keepers of the earth, the planters of the seed (both earthly and otherwise). Most important with regard to spirituality, men are quicker to purify their souls because they are *less* tied to earthly, bodily functions. They do not menstruate, give birth, or lactate for that matter, freeing them up to focus on intellectual or divine matters. The goal of the well-lived religious life has usually involved *triumph* over the body, and for thousands of years men have seen themselves as having bodies more adept at this battle. As a result, men have also traditionally regarded themselves as more spiritual or better suited to represent God (v. convenient as they've held all the power to determine these things), while concluding that women are more earthy in their bodily capacities and thus not worthy enough for this honor. Under patriarchy, this has led *both men and women* to support the notion that the male body and masculine language are most fitting to represent the divine, leading to what feminist theologian Sandra Schneiders describes as "a paralysis of the religious imagination" in how we talk about and picture the divine.

If we are to begin imagining the female body, be that the body of a Bridget Jones, a Cannie Shapiro, or ourselves as the body of a contemporary goddess, then we are going to have to do some chucking in the God-image department. Together with Bridget, and by drawing from some of the many women today who are re-imagining the divine, we can work toward letting go of this traditional God-image (v. cathartic in manner of enjoying martini as way of releasing stress post-workday). In order for us to find the goddess in Bridget and, ultimately, the goddess in ourselves, we need to think of the divine in terms of *becoming* (not only being), of *desiring* (not empty of desire), of *evolving,* as we, too, evolve as persons throughout the journeys of our lives. This will take an act of daring imagination on our part (as urged by Dr. Schneiders), not to mention possibly offending the male monopoly on how we are *supposed* to think and talk about God.

Breaking Up with God Is Hard to Do (but v. therapeutic)

~

Step Number One: Think of Him and Then Try to Forget Him

The first thing we need to do as we try and locate the Girlie Feminine Divine is wipe away that image of Father God as old-man-wizard-Gandalf-in-the-sky. I am guessing here that if I asked you to picture God in your heads, something like this kind of image immediately pops up. (Personally, now having seen *Lord of the Rings,* this is how I picture the God I grew up with: old man, long white beard, very tall, sitting on cloud—however, not galloping on horse). This Man-God usually comes with the following qualities: all-powerful, omniscient, forgiving-yet-punishing, distant, and, ultimately, *immutable.* (Or, as I like to call Him, *stagnant.* Totally inhuman. Far away. *Boring.*) OK, so get ready to chuck this Man (at least for now).

Step Number Two: Use Male-Designed Tradition for Womanly Liberating Purposes

While we are traditionally taught to personify Allah, YHWH, and the Trinitarian God of Christianity (Father, Son, and Holy Spirit) as Male in manner of Gandalf, these traditions also teach that our personification of God is *always* metaphorical. In other words, using the human to image God can never capture God fully. This is because, while humans are fallible, imperfect, immortal creatures, God is unchanging and perfect and totally transcends (exists apart from) the world. (Isn't it funny, though, how in our religious upbringing, somehow the metaphorical part of the whole "Father God" thing was conveniently left out, leaving us to think that God is *really* a man? Hmmm.) On the one hand we learn to divorce spirituality from the human body: God is ethereal, disembodied, a force around us, rather than something that we can touch, as the human body could never accurately represent the divine. (All v. unfortunate if you're hoping that the spiritual life and touching Mr. Darcy have something in common.) But at the same time we also learn to associate the *male body* as the most appropriate image to represent God (so perhaps touching Mr. Darcy is much like touching God, Himself, which I suppose is an improvement).

> *Without our bodies to help us, we would be lost in our endeavors to imagine the divine, and it is about time for us to see women's bodies as worthy of representing the divine.*

Yet viewing God as transcendent in nature has also become a blessing in disguise within certain circles of women. For many feminist theologians, both Christian and Jewish, the emphasis on historical images of God as *always* metaphorical has led them to ask, "If our language and images of God are *truly* metaphorical, then why not personify God as a woman?" (Hurrah! V. sneaky, these women.) Scholar Rita Gross claims that the feminine personification of YHWH in the Jewish tradition is actually a *mitzvah,* or obligation, for the Jewish people. Doing so reunites the feminine aspects of the divine that have *always* been a part of Judaism but hidden behind the masculine God that is consistently, publicly celebrated. Other scholars have imaged God as Mother, as birth-giver to creation, as Wisdom-Sophia, as caregiver to humanity, and even going so far as to imagine Jesus in feminine terms within Christianity.

Step Number Three: Take Things Even Further (which is why we are at step three)

Building on the idea that all language and images about God are metaphorical—the metaphor being used to introduce a woman's body and feminine language as a legitimate way to imagine the divine—has been quite transformative for many women (scholars at least). But much of this work still supports an idea of God that is unchangeable, perfect, and transcendent—a faraway divine that conforms to the patriarchal ideas that have dominated for thousands of years. If we are going to re-imagine the divine in women like Bridget, who is definitely not operating outside this world, then using feminine language and images to think about the divine hovering (in manner of hover-craft) somewhere far away isn't going to suffice. Lucky for us, there are lots of other women scholars of religion (Carol Christ, Grace Jantzen, and Dorothee Soelle, to name three) who have argued that what we need is a god or goddess who *changes,* who needs, who relates to us—a vulnerable divine, *not* a god who is distant, unfeeling, and disembodied. As humanity is vulnerable, evolving, loving, and needing to receive love as embodied creatures, so we need to imagine a divine who encompasses these experiences and evolves with us. Seeking a feminine-divine-in-process has led Carol Christ, for example, to write urgently and prolifically that women *need* a goddess—one that helps us love our bodies *as* divine, seeing our bodily processes, changes, struggles, and pleasures as representative of the goddess in all of us.

Step Number Four: Let Go of Him!

If we are going to look at bodies like those of Cannie and Bridget (and our own) as appropriate models for the divine, then we have to let go of this perfected-God image that we've inherited. These women are not perfect, and neither are we. Letting go of God as "out there," up in the sky, all-knowing, and unchanging is difficult in many respects, because the psychology of this image for many of us is powerful and deep. Most of us automatically think of absolute knowledge and perfection when we hear the word *god* or talk of the divine. But as we pursue Inner Poise, our capacity to see (or not see) the divine expressed in the female body, regardless of its shape, size, appearance (and choice of shoes), depends on our ability to *get past* this past (and unburdening ourselves of this image will make us feel lighter in manner of miracle weight-loss yet without having to change eating habits which is v.v.g.).

A Goddess Who Counts Calories, Plucks Her Eyebrows, and Paints Her Toenails

~

In the movie version of *Bridget Jones's Diary* we literally see Bridget go from dowdy-and-down to desirable-and-daring, unafraid to show her full-bodied self in all of its glory (and poundage). She is certainly not a vision of tragedy or sadness but instead alive with humor and self-awareness. We see the same transformation happen in Cannie Shapiro when, after she slims herself down to the point where people regard her as skinny, she realizes that in a skinny body she no longer feels like herself. What's *healthy* on a spiritual level about these women's journeys in relation to their bodies, despite their ups and downs, is that we can't separate our images of Bridget and Cannie from their bodies. Nor should we try (or perhaps they would become ghosts?). With regard to Bridget in particular, whether it is through relentless calorie counting, exclaiming "hurrah!" joyously when she loses a pound or two, or accidentally revealing her backside to all of London, Bridget's sense of self is inextricably tied to her experience of being embodied as a woman. The body, for Bridget, is alternately a source of pain and joy, an object of beauty and despair—something she wishes in one moment to hide and at another to reveal in a glorious, mind-boggling shag. Without our bodies to help us, we would be lost in our endeavors to imagine the divine, and it is about time for us to see women's bodies as worthy of representing the divine (in all our beauty, style, and, alternately, frustration).

Inner Poise is not about achieving "perfection," whatever that means (perhaps should ask male for appropriate
definition?). Nor does it require us to relinquish our calorie
counting or the desire to achieve a particular standard of
beauty. Seeing ourselves as goddesses need not require us to
stop shaving our legs, changing our look, or engaging in our
morning beauty regimens in order to perpetuate the idea that
seeing the divine in ourselves means we must *already* be
perfect (and because as we all know that shaving legs is
rather essential for optimum short-skirt wearing). There is no
one ideal for all women's bodies nor *one* definition of what
it means to be beautiful. All women are different; no woman
is perfect, and, inevitably, how we envision what our bodies
could be and should be will change over the course of our
lifetime. We have different skin colors, body shapes, fashion
senses, and relationships to our bodies. Some of us are more
comfortable with a more naturalistic style of body and beauty,
and some of us take joy in plucking, primping, and stylizing
our looks for hours at a time. A woman is no less a goddess
if she counts her calories, paints her toenails, and dresses in
a way that celebrates her curves than someone who does not.
Thus creating a *single* divine image, already formed, already
perfected for us to aspire to ceases to make sense in the face
of our diversity.

The spiritual life is often about self-transformation,
about being reborn again and again; for women, the body can
be a source of transformation and rebirth on many levels. We
transform the body through exercise and reinvent our appearance with what we wear from one day to the next. Becoming

a Goddess of Inner Poise involves our capacity to imagine ourselves as different, as transformed, as reborn, as beautiful—
and as vulnerable and imperfect as well. A Goddess of Inner
Poise can be emotional about her body, despairing when she
does not live up to her expectations but also exclaiming in
utter joy and self-praise (in manner of praising our Inner Divine) when she triumphs. As women, we care about our bodies, care about beauty, and often use fashion to express who
we are in the moment, transforming ourselves from one image
to another by putting on an outfit, much as if we are putting
on a new self. Like our heroine Bridget, the key to Inner Poise
is to take the plunge into self-reflection to figure out how we
experience our own bodies. It involves remaining good-
humored and aware of our struggles, hoping to *eventually* love
our bodies as they are (mostly) but also celebrating our capacity, like Bridget, to reincarnate ourselves through our bodies and relish the Girlie Feminine Divine in all of us.

4

"Forgive Us Our Trespasses!"

When It Comes to Vice, We Shall Flourish as Tulips!

Deadly sins committed by Bridget: 7 (v. bad as includes all). Deadly sins committed by me: at least 1 (v. gluttonous as consuming chocolate in shocking amounts). Remedies for haphazard sinning behavior: confession (v.g. as Bridget esp. good at it). Positive thoughts about confessing: many (as confessing transforms dirty, sinful self into beautiful blooming tulip!).

Celebrating with Toffee and Other Punishable Behavior

~

Perhaps Bridget's evil boss Daniel says it best in response to a typical Bridget lapse in willpower. Post-consumption of twelve alcohol units, as confessed by Bridget (which apparently adds up to three bottles of champagne), she is getting sick in the "loo" in a rather unbecoming drunken stupor. When she tries to hide this embarrassment from Daniel (albeit unsuccessfully), he calls out to her in mock seriousness: "There goes your inner poise, my plumptious. Best place for it, I say." So much for Bridget's virtuous endeavors to curb alcohol consumption, among other excesses, as Inner Poise seems to disappear down the toilet rather quickly.

Though Bridget's central indulgences appear to be alcohol units and possibly cigarettes of the *Silk Cut* variety (v. bad), she verges on countless others in her many struggles. She is so forthcoming in confessing life's little vices that we can easily expand her list of transgressions to include

1. Never cleaning her flat (v. slothful)
2. Enjoying impure thoughts about various men and nights of shagging (v. lustful)
3. Buying and hoarding needless objects and lottery tickets (v. greedy)
4. Consuming large quantities of Cadbury Milk Tray (v. gluttonous)
5. Feeling satisfied with self due to weight loss (v. prideful)
6. Exclaiming endlessly about emotional dysfunctions of men (v. angry)
7. Being catty with friends about manipulative, Darcy-stealing Rebecca (v. envious)

All of the above "issues" are readily apparent from the moment we meet Bridget in the *Diary* through her extensive New Year's resolution listing of "I Wills" and "I Will Nots." As with her relentless calorie counting, Bridget makes no secret of what some might call her shameless sinful behavior—flirting with all the seven deadlies in a matter of a few pages (v. impressive).

Whereas Bridget flirts with alcohol, at the top of my indulgence list is chocolate, so I am probably most guilty of *gluttony* as far as deadly sins go. Much like Ms. Jones, I operate on a reward-punishment system when it comes to my consumption rituals. I even have a special category of chocolates that falls under the heading "celebration," as in *Celebration Toffee* (C.T.): a joy-inspired creation from my favorite chocolate heaven, Vosges. At least in my life, it is important to have a stash of this extremely buttery substance coated in chocolate and nutty yum-myness in case cause for celebration arises unexpectedly. Upon advent of said cause, I am given permission (because the gods are clearly smiling on me at this moment) to "celebrate" by replacing a healthy, body-nourishing meal with an entire box of C.T. in manner of Mardi Gras, pre-Lent, pagan-like festival.

> Though the Chicks of Chick Lit may not be traipsing to church to unburden their souls to a man in a dress, there is spiritual possibility rooted in their unique and humorous confessional style.

Of course, there is sometimes a downside to my excesses. Like a post-drunken stupor that Bridget later bemoans, I am known to wallow in sugar-induced comas (though in bed, not in loo) for upwards of several hours post–Vosges C.T. binge. It is the coma that lets me know that, in fact, I have misinterpreted the divine-smiling thing, and the gods instead are punishing me for my transgressions. (But, in the end, am willing to withstand minor smiting, as chocolate so delicious, smiting totally worth it.)

So Many Sins, So Little Time!
(so many shoes, so little money!)

~

Whether it's eating couture chocolates in excess or consuming far too many alcohol units, there are seemingly infinite ways to sin within Western religion, and our heroines of Chick Lit are no strangers to sinful behavior. In the Catholic tradition, a faith known for wallowing on about sin with a Bridget-like caliber, there are two major categories of sin: the venial and the mortal. Venial sins are the more forgivable kind and include activities such as spending money on lottery tickets, telling what we might call white lies, or even consuming a bit too much chocolate one afternoon. Much of Bridget's sinning falls under the category of the venial (hurrah! sinful tendencies are in fact v. minor and forgivable).

Of course, venial sins *can* cross the line to become the mortal variety if taken to utter extremes. Mortal sins involve transgressions of "Ten Commandments" proportions: idolatry, adultery, stealing, coveting, committing murder, and of course any of the seven deadly sins. These are the sins to watch out for, and when it comes to the commandment about how "thou shall not covet," we all might be in a bit of trouble (the kind of trouble that sends us into fiery hellish places in manner of Dante's *Inferno*).

Like Bridget, so many of us covet all manner of things, from fashionable items to cigarettes to men. When it comes to fashion, *Shopaholic*'s Becky Bloomwood might be the reigning queen in the coveting department. There is virtually nothing material that escapes her gaze, and at one point she waxes on about her regrettable neglect of an entire category of items: luggage. To make up for this dreadful oversight on her part, she vows to give special attention to, ahem, *luggage,* to make up for previous wrongful behavior. I am not quite sure rectifying past neglect by purchasing large amounts of baggage is really drawing her any closer to becoming a virtuous girl, much as that sounds like a wonderful idea (that our virtue could be wrapped up in purchasing items across all areas of fashion, ensuring that we do not neglect any one area lest it feel left out).

While we are on the subject of cardinal sinning, I may as well mention the adultery thing, which also might pose a problem for Bridget and her fellow Chick heroines, since having sex with someone if you are unmarried is actually considered adultery. (The man you are cheating on in this situation: God "Himself"! V. kinky weird idea but will get to that topic in next chapter.)

Beyond categorizing sin according to the mortal and venial, sinful behavior is often understood as an obstacle standing in the way of our spiritual life and growth. In other words, sin involves activity, be it intentional or unintentional, whose end result separates us from the divine and diverts us from our spiritual path. In Judaism, sin is traditionally understood as an act of rebellion—an intentional betrayal of the Law—and therefore worthy of divine punishment. In both the Christian and Jewish traditions, turning away from God leads to the aimless wandering of humanity in a state of darkness, as the Israelites wandered lost in the desert for forty years following the Exodus from Egypt. (Perhaps in much the same way we wander aimlessly in Barney's, lovingly feeling fabrics and trying on fashions we cannot afford, risking exposure to blinding prices and making us desperately thirsty for a raise.) On the Eastern side of things, within Hinduism one must earn good Karma or risk coming back in another life as a member of a lower caste, or worse, as a bug of some sort. The concept and consequences of reincarnation are meant to inspire one to a life of virtue, but also exact a kind of payback for those intensely prone to making poor choices (v. scary sounding, indeed).

Reality Spirituality: Why Confession Is Cleansing (and can make skin baby soft!)

~

Between forty years of Israeli wandering, God's requirement that Jesus be crucified to "pay" for the collective sins of humanity, and a Hindu's worry about whether "a bug's life" is in store for the future, the road to forgiveness can sound rather harsh and possibly dry-skin-inducing. I must admit that I have never been the biggest fan of labeling myself a *sinner* either (or anyone else for that matter) and usually refrain from using the term altogether. Nor do I buy into the more extreme view that forgiveness is totally out of our hands—a popular Protestant Christian idea. The notion that we can do nothing for forgiveness arises out of an extremely distant and rather severe understanding of the divine, since in many traditions God acts the part of the all-knowing, all-watching Father figure in manner of the Freudian uber-Dad—difficult to please and unpredictable in how He doles out justice, punishment, and grace.

(Interpretation: All the kindness in the world may never make up for alcohol units consumed by Bridget.) The Freudian uber-Dad-God should sound familiar, since He is the same God we worked at chucking in the last chapter.

Yet in thinking about the role of vice and virtue in relation to our spiritual journeys, I do find it helpful to reflect on the notion of sin as something that "gets in the way" of the Inner Poise we hope to achieve in our lives. Recalling the image of Bridget's Inner Poise disappearing down the loo despite all her efforts or Becky's purchase of yet another high-priced item just after she resolves to cut back is enough not only to make us laugh and cringe but also to show how our habits can become obstacles to our spiritual growth. Sin understood in this way is something that stands in the way of our becoming the women we know we *could* be. It can affect our relationships

> *Inner Poise does not have to be about becoming perfect, relinquishing all (in manner of cloistering self from world), and feeling utter guilt and despair when we fall short of our hopes or enjoy one martini too many.*

and influence our overall ability to lead fulfilling, happy lives (as receiving letters from debt collectors on a weekly basis certainly does not move one quickly along the path of spiritual growth). And, as Becky realizes toward the end of *Shopaholic,* failure to face her transgressions is not only painful on a personal level but can end up hurting others around her, even if unintentionally. These "habits" we struggle to get under control can not only affect our personal journeys but can have a negative effect on our communities as well (really hindering resolutions like Bridget's to "be kinder to others").

Despite the numerous excesses of the Bridgets and Beckys of fiction and their unending struggle to get them in check, the intense honesty we see in their characters already sets them on the path to virtue (v.g. news). I mentioned in Chapter One about journaling as a spiritually significant act, that the stories of Bridget, Becky, and even teenager Mia Thermopolis of Meg Cabot's *The Princess Diaries,* are framed as *confessions*. Confessing in manner of spelling out (literally, on the written page) their attempts to tame excesses, sometimes successfully, sometimes not so much, gives these characters a space in life where they can own up to their struggles, no matter how grave or embarrassing. Though the Chicks of Chick Lit may not be traipsing to church to unburden their souls to a man in a dress, there is spiritual possibility rooted in their unique and humorous confessional style. And as it happens, the practice of confession as a means to finding forgiveness and grace, reuniting ourselves with the divine, and atoning for our shortcomings has a long history within religion (and our fictional goddesses are practically experts at it already!).

Originally, confession served a therapeutic or cathartic purpose that allowed early Christians to unburden themselves of their sinful thoughts as a kind of release, in much the same way that we approach therapy today (but much cheaper). In *The Confessions* of St. Augustine, he is rather extreme in his willingness to confess every detail he found deplorable about himself (he counts sins like Bridget counts calories). Even the most minor transgressions he found exceedingly important and essential to include (and as far as itemizing transgressions go, it is possible that Augustine and Bridget are v. distant cousins). Within the Jewish tradition, the ten days between Rosh Hashanah and Yom Kippur (which literally translates to Day of Atonement) mark the annual Jewish period of repentance from sin. On Rosh Hashanah, the "book of life" opens, and one begins reflecting and asking for forgiveness for all of the last year's transgressions until Yom Kippur, the day when the book of life officially closes. (If Bridget were Jewish, Yom Kippur might turn out to be her scariest time of year, as she might not have enough time to atone for all transgressions before Book of Life closes. Would be quite a race against clock.)

Within traditional religion, the practice of owning up to a life filled with vice, via the confessing of transgressions, and the resolve to get our not-so-positive habits in check has a cleansing effect on us. It is a means of beginning anew or *emptying* the self (literally for some Christians)—a kind of rebirth. By opening up to our deeper selves through confession, we open up to a divine intimacy previously unavailable to us, as sinful habits come between us and a positive relationship with the divine (i.e. Inner Poise). Cleansing the self in this way allows for a kind of Hindu-style reincarnation, just without the *literal* dying part. Many Christians who describe themselves as "born again" talk of a "dying" of the old, sinful self, who was lost to God, and "putting on" a new self—one that is filled with God's grace. (Perhaps dying of old, sinful self begets new, slender, sexy self in manner of goddess-like supermodel!

Perhaps must try to become born again in manner of Evangelical Christian! Or maybe not as then would have to give up shagging.)

Yet in a famous critique of the Christian doctrines of sin and love, scholar Valerie Saiving argues that the traditional definitions of sin as pride and desire and of love as total self-lessness, or emptying of the self, only lead us to become an empty shell of a person. A life lived *without* a measure of what she calls "divine discontent"—a discontent that leads us to transform ourselves throughout life, to embark on adventure, to learn, to question, to discover what it means to be a better person—is an unfulfilled life; rather than making us more virtuous, it instead leads us toward an unfulfilling, "unflourishing life" (more on this in a minute). Saiving hoped to transform our understanding of virtue from selflessness to become a kind of divine engagement, or dialogue, with the world and others—a conversation that I see prominently in the novels of Chick Lit (hurrah! Our struggles with vice-like habit are practically conversations with god!).

We Are Much Like Perennials (preferably of the tulip variety as v. pretty and sleek)

~

While we *can* root our heroines' compulsion to confess in the ground of traditional religion, what this foundation nurtures in them is not a perpetual wallowing in how impossibly sinful they will always be, in manner of St. Augustine himself (v.g. as Augustine never gets over himself—ever). Their intense self-reflections, evaluations, and determinations regarding what they must do to achieve Inner Poise and spiritual epiphany (as Bridget would say) lead to a far more positive-thought-filled perspective on the whole redemption-salvation issue, toward more of a divine engagement, as Saiving might call it. In fact, their confession-style reflections are not so much about their *need* for salvation or redemption in manner of Jesus-having-to-sacrifice-self-to-redeem-humanity at all. Rather, as they struggle to become better, kinder persons with Inner Poise, the kind of spiritual value we see expressed in their confessions fits better with cutting-edge feminist philosophy and spirituality than with religious notions of redemption (hurrah! Chick-style confessing is edgy scholarly effort in manner of professor at Oxford! v. respectable).

In *Becoming Divine,* British scholar Grace Jantzen gives a thorough critique of Western religion's obsession with salvation. The problem with salvation, according to Jantzen, is that it "denotes rescue. One is saved from something: from drowning, from calamity, from loss." (OK, maybe so far salvation seems like a necessary item for Bridget as she faces many calamities and for Becky who is drowning in debt, but stay with me.) Salvation has negative connotations and implies that we are lacking something (i.e. inner goodness) and are in need of something *outside* of us to fix or fill what is missing (again, our inner goodness). So the need to be saved or redeemed places goodness and grace outside of us rather than within us in such a way that our self-image cannot benefit positively. As a response to this problem, Jantzen proposes that as we struggle with ourselves, our hopes, and our shortcomings, rather than ask for redemption we instead should seek to *flourish:* "A movement or person 'in full-flourish' is a movement or person that is vibrant and creative, blossoming and developing and coming to fruition." (Yessss! Struggles with habit and vice can lead to blossoming of self in manner of lovely tulip!)

In many ways, Bridget's striving toward Inner Poise *is* her attempt to flourish in manner of what Grace Jantzen is talking about: seeking Inner Poise is about a healing and growth that comes from within, not from some force wholly outside our being (and beyond anyone's being for that matter). In all the heroines of Chick Lit, we find struggle, setback, and resolve to try again (even when all seems lost and the bank won't stop calling). But perhaps most important, in the Chick style of confessing we not only see acute self-aware-

> Despite the numerous excesses of the Bridgets and Beckys of fiction . . . the intense honesty we see in their characters already sets them on the path to virtue (v.g. news).

ness and evaluation in these women but we find a sense of virtue *within themselves as well as in those around them*. Despite ups, downs, and excesses, the women of Chick Lit are neither blind to seeing the good within or to helping *others* identify their own virtues, reaching out to their friends when they can't manage alone. For Jantzen, seeking to flourish is not a solitary endeavor either. As a flower is rooted in the earth, needing the soil, air, and life all around it to thrive (not to mention that each flower has its own way of "giving back" to the earth that nourishes it), to flourish as humans we need supportive community on many levels, and in flourishing ourselves we participate in our community's thriving. The flourishing that is Inner Poise is not something "out there" beyond our reach; it is instead something within and all around us—the Inner Poise that doesn't disappear down the loo but a divine engagement or "discontent" that stays with us as we reach toward and grasp moments of goodness and empowerment.

While we are on the subject of flourishing and its role in a larger community, we must acknowledge that the vast majority of Chick heroines do limit their sphere of communal engagement to themselves and their immediate surroundings; flourishing generally extends only as far as their nearest and dearest. The "Bridget in All of Us" would do well to take a nod from any of Meg Cabot's wonderful heroines, both young (teenagers!) and older (twenty-somethings). (But should remember here that Bridget is practically teenager at heart, just residing in the body of a thirty-something Singleton.) Cabot's characters, like Mia Thermopolis from *The Princess Diaries,* Samantha Madison from *All-American Girl,* and Melissa Fuller from *Boy Next Door,* all have something in common in the flourishing department: a call to giving back that extends *beyond* their immediate loved ones. In Melissa Fuller, we see the ideal good neighbor (in NYC no less). Throughout the *Princess Diaries,* we encounter in Mia not only a girl who romanticizes about Hollywood Hotties but also a political activist and environmentalist who spends her spring breaks doing projects like Housing for the Hopeful. Samantha Madison (after saving the president from assassination) has the opportunity to make a powerful political statement in her role as the U.S. Teen Diplomat to the U.N.

and stands up for her beliefs against immense pressure not to. I think Jantzen would agree that if we are to understand Inner Poise as flourishing, eventually as we stretch toward this horizon we must stretch beyond our regular comfort zones and communities to learn what it means to nourish and be nourished by the world beyond our immediate doorstep.

So Inner Poise à la flourishing is not a one-stop spiritual epiphany, a single experience of rebirth, or a prayer for rescue. It is, rather, a many-step process of ups and downs, births and rebirths (i.e. in manner of perennial!), initiated within and nourished by those around us. It involves a willingness to look inside ourselves and honestly explore our desires—the ones that lead us to compromising positions, be that in the loo or in our bank accounts. Inner Poise requires us not only to discover our temptations but to struggle continuously, as does Bridget, to fulfill the goals we have set for ourselves, celebrating the many moments of rebirth we achieve along the way. Inner Poise does not have to be about becoming perfect, relinquishing all (in manner of cloistering self from world), and feeling utter guilt and despair when we fall short of our hopes or enjoy one martini too many. Instead, Inner Poise leaves room for loving the self (at times in manner of chocolate treats); it *includes* room for forgiveness when we fall short of our hopes and *makes room* for new desires to flourish within us, freeing us up for a creative engagement with the world that is fitting of the Goddesses of Inner Poise we hope to become.

5

"Am Irresistible Sex Goddess! Hurrah!"

When Shagging and Snogging Are Divine

Calories burned during shagging: probably millions (v.g.). Positive thoughts about shagging: infinite (as excellent weight-loss program). Fool-proof strategies for ensuring night of wild shagging: 1 (just wear hideous grandma knickers on a date). Religious complications regarding Singleton shagging: best not to count—

"Shag me! Shag me!" (Yessss! Yessss!)

Aside from recent Christian spin-off Chick Lit novels like Kristin Billerbeck's *What a Girl Wants: A Novel* that tout protagonists who drink less, worry about virginity, and are looking for a good Christian man, for the vast majority of our heroines there seems to be nothing better than a night of shagging. (Though I must also say it *does* depend on their mood, since a good sample sale might tide Becky Bloomwood over for a while, a few alcohol units and some chocolate might satisfy Bridget temporarily, and selling a screenplay might do

if you are Cannie Shapiro.) While there may be a new trend
out there in Chick fiction labeled "Bridget Jones goes to
church," Helen Fielding's Bridget may indeed go to church if
there is a wedding involved, but she'd better watch out that
she doesn't burst into flames when she arrives (in manner of
all-consuming hellfire). Bridget and all of her friends (both
straight and gay) spend a good deal of time thinking about
shagging, talking about shagging, wondering when the next
opportunity to shag will arise, looking for shagging prospects,
and then, of course, having a good shag whenever the occasion presents itself.

Our silver-screen Bridget seems especially lucky
when it comes to sex, as she gets both boss Daniel (Hugh
Grant) and Mark Darcy (Colin Firth) into bed in just under
two hours! (What girl could resist that kind of sex-goddess
opportunity?) In the Chick Lit shagging department, I think
Bridget might be the reigning queen, both in terms of number of occasions *and* amount of commentary, excitement,
and humor expressed in response to said occasions (as Bridget shows great emotion regarding sex: both joy and frustration between shags). Tom, Shazzer, and Jude are not exactly
practicing celibacy either, and for Bridget and friends a shag-
filled life is a happy life. Even the Smug Marrieds, at the same
time they are lording their permanent relationship status over
their Singleton counterparts, look wistfully on as Bridget and
company make the most of their sexual freedom.

I have yet to read a Chick novel (at least of the adult
variety) that doesn't include its heroine shagging at least
one man, and many of these stories pivot on exactly *when*
each heroine will finally get the opportunity for the long-

anticipated event. While our Singleton heroines shag with wild abandon, their teenager counterparts like Mia Thermopolis (*The Princess Diaries*), Samantha Madison (*All-American Girl*), and Georgie Nicolson (*Angus, Thongs, and Full-Frontal Snogging* by Louise Renison) are just as interested in snogging: who, when, where, how? (All v. important questions if you are a teenage girl.) In anticipation of the long-awaited shag while reading, it is difficult to stop from thinking, "Yessss! Yessss!" when Becky Bloomwood finally gets Luke Brandon's shirt off, when Cannie discovers (and enjoys) love in an unlikely suitor after suffering her ex's jerky behavior for ages, and when Melissa Fuller finally "gets things right" with John Trent. For these women, having sex is a goal, experiencing sex is joyful, and, while occasionally pain and frustration are attributed to it (if one is chucked after sex or if one is not able to obtain it) and aside from Cannie Shapiro's complicated consequences from a one-night mistake, sex is a virtual Mecca for the starlets of Chick fiction.

First, the Bad News: Why Sex Is a Religio-Political Quagmire for Women

~

There is little doubt that the premarital, shag-filled escapades of Bridget, Becky, Cannie, Melissa, Kate Mackenzie (list could go on but must stop somewhere) go far outside the boundaries of what's acceptable within religious sexual morality. While the bedroom adventures of our heroines on the printed page, as well as on *Sex and the City* and *Friends*, make sense for the contemporary Singleton lifestyle (as abstaining from sex for the majority of adult life seems archaic and out

of the question), the practice is relatively impossible to reconcile with traditional religion. (As religions are generally not
interested in making *sense,* rather, prefer to remain *timeless,*
i.e. irrelevant to how people are actually living their lives at
this particular *time,* particularly if you are a woman.)

In *The Good News About Sex and Marriage,* Catholic
writer Christopher West affirms some rather bad news about
sex for Singleton folk (rather ironically, given the title). According to West, premarital sex equals selfish gratification and occurs absolutely apart from love; it's sinful through and through, even if we are engaged to be Smug Married (rather harsh, isn't he?). Though "luckily," if we've already blown it and given up our virginity, West claims that the good news is that Christ will forgive us if we renounce our evil sinful ways (so there's hope, I guess?).

> *To expect single people who are waiting longer and longer to get married . . . to deny ourselves as sexual beings until well into our thirties and forties is, for most of us, simply an unrealistic and outdated expectation.*

Unless we go back to ancient goddess traditions that
sanctioned the ritualized, nonmarital shag to celebrate the arrival of spring (Marion Zimmer Bradley's feminist version of
the King Arthur legend *The Mists of Avalon* is a great read on
the subject), each religion more or less expresses the same
sentiments about sinful sex as West: unless you are Smug Mar-

ried, you must guard your purity *at all costs*. The responsibility for adulterous acts, as well as the preservation of virginity, is traditionally placed on the female sex in *both* Western and Eastern religions. Preserving one's virginity for the sanctity of marriage is supposed to be our highest goal as women, and punishable by pain of death in some traditions if we do not (not kidding here).

For men and women in Hinduism, Buddhism, and Jainism (though men are considered more adept at this), a life of perpetual virginity is prized well above the married life, as denial of bodily desire is the ultimate achievement. Women in these traditions are generally considered less suited for virginity, however, as they are more prone to lust (talk about male projection of their own desires on women) and temptresses placed on earth to lure men into sex and therefore sinful behavior. (In the Muslim faith, there are "ten parts" to desire, and women represent nine!) Should a woman fail to remain pure, she not only risks shame on herself but in many traditions (especially in Islam and Orthodox Judaism) she can destroy her future marriage prospects, as well as bring dishonor and shame on her family. In the Muslim tradition, sex outside marriage, even in cases of rape, can doom a woman forever, not to mention endanger her life (v. depressing, indeed). Though interestingly, *within* Jewish and Islamic marriage the human experience of the erotic *is* valued but only *within* the boundaries of marriage (and usually at the whim of the man, not the woman). (So, no matter what tradition you are, Singleton shagging is just out of the question. V. disappointing. Am thinking possibly there is no hope for the out-of-wedlock shag that promotes spiritual growth. Hhhmmmm.)

Last bit of depressing news I'll share about our sexual escapades: Singleton shagging not only can ruin a woman's purity and Smug Marital opportunities, but also violates the Ten Commandments about how "thou shall not commit adultery." You may wonder here: If I am not married, then how am I committing adultery by having sex? Well, within Christianity, adultery is not just about cheating on your spouse, since in *pre*marital sex one is cheating on *God* (as until a woman pledges herself to a man, she is pledged to the God-Man), and in *extra*marital sex a woman violates *both* the human man and the divinely sanctioned vow. Of course, the double standard regarding sexual morality thrives across world religions, and the imbalance is clear: Islam, Judaism, and Christianity are always more forgiving of the promiscuous male who seeks sexual satisfaction outside wedlock, be it premarital or extramarital. In *The Woman in the Balcony: On Rereading the Song of Songs,* Daphne Merkin comments that within Judaism: "If a man can't handle his urges, advises the Talmud, he should go to a neighboring town and seek relief." (What?!) This kind of advice shouldn't shock us though, since even in our relatively promiscuous Western "freedom," the responsibility on the female for sex is codified in secular culture as well; we all know that the promiscuous male gets pats on the back while the promiscuous female is labeled a slut (not v. nice at all).

Officially Approved Shagging Options for Singletons: Zero (v. unforgiving)

~

None of the above is surprise news that I am announcing, though it is certainly depressing as far as spirituality goes and a rather different picture of sex from the one we get from the authors and heroines of Chick Lit. To sum things up, within traditional religion our options regarding shagging seem restricted to the following:

1. Convince self that self is *asexual* in manner of amoeba for decades upon decades until God reveals soul mate to us in divine vision and we get Smug Married.
2. Get Smug Married at age eighteen in manner of Mum and Dad to first bloke that comes around so we can shag with "official" permission like good little girlies.
3. If gay or lesbian, remain celibate for entirety of life, again in manner of amoeba, while trying to convince self to ignore true sexual orientation and join the ranks of Smug Marrieds.
4. Shag with wild abandon regardless of sexual orientation, and keep pesky religion out of our sex lives. What God doesn't know (and Mum and Dad for that matter), won't hurt God! (Best option, I say.)
5. Become "A New Celibate" (a born-again virgin)!

Born-again virginity, or "The New Celibacy" as Bridget calls it, is a rather popular fad among certain men and women who are either Evangelical Christians who've had sex and renounced their former evil, sinful ways, or with people who have had plenty of sex but have decided that they've had enough sex for now and will now wait for future sex with a "permanent" significant other. At one point, even our sex goddess Bridget swears off shagging and decides she will practice this New Celibacy, deciding that she will *not* shag in the future. Of course, she advocates this practice only as a result of a dry spell in her sex life. She quickly renounces her decision when shagging Mark Darcy again becomes an option (who wouldn't?).

Aside from this rare detour or two among our heroines regarding the question to shag or not to shag, Bridget, Becky, Cannie, Melissa, and everyone else are happily choosing option number 4 from the list as their preferred approach to sex. Those of us who see our choices about sex as similar to Bridget's are in a unique situation, since many of our parents (dare I say most, minus the flower children) are each other's one-and-only, and that was *after* they married each other (practically while they were still teenagers). While most of us growing up with post-sixties free love have been schooled in traditional religious rules about sex, most of us have also chosen to ignore these rules in much the same manner as our fictional girls, going happily about enjoying our Singleton shagging (v. subversive, but I'll get to that later). To expect single people who are waiting longer and longer to get married, if we choose to marry at all, to deny ourselves as sexual beings until well into our thirties and forties is, for most of us, simply an unrealistic and outdated expectation. The truly innocent woman in white walking down the aisle is a rarity today, though most women wear the traditional white dress anyway (as white is often very becoming color, highlighting skin tone). The preservation of sexual innocence for decades upon decades takes the kind of willpower and ascetic discipline of Olympian-quality virgins, and it is simply a practice or "goal" that the Carrie Bradshaw generation of women does not value in the same way as our parents, priests, ministers, and rabbis *still* do.

As grown women, *we are having sex* as Singletons, and regardless of what religious teachings may say about it, we know that sex can be just as good and loving outside of marriage as within it. More important for our discussion about spirituality: as the generation changing the waters as far as our sense of sexual freedom goes, an unfortunate complication we face regarding religion's blanket prohibition on premarital sex is that we end up learning to disassociate our spiritual lives from our sexuality as we go about

> *We are having sex as Singletons, and regardless of what religious teachings may say about it, we know that sex can be just as good and loving outside of marriage as within it.*

breaking the rules. Even Bridget expresses this distinction (between spirituality and sex) when she comments, "Look, am not supposed to be thinking about sex. Am spiritual." Despite our spiritual cravings, whether consciously or not the religious notion that sex is *only* sacred within marriage weighs heavily on our experiences. Somewhere tucked away in our minds, our conscience is reminding us that Smug Marriage is considered the only acceptable "container" for our lustful ways, so the easiest solution is to divorce our spiritual pursuits from our sexual ones (in the same way that we often learn to disassociate spirituality with our bodies in general).

So where then do we go for refuge regarding sex and the Singleton spiritual life? Outside of Smug Marrieddom, is having sex really as awful as traditional religion portrays it to be? Is it truly an act of adultery against God? A cardinal sin that will doom us to hell unless we repent? Or is there another way of seeing things that we've been missing? Unfortunately, regarding Singleton shagging and its spiritual potential, we are simply out of luck if our hope is to find a spiritual home that actually *condones* our sexuality outside of Smug Married life. It simply does not exist, so we will have to think outside traditional parameters here (since our sexuality already stands outside of them anyway). Though I will warn that, unless we all decide that The New Celibacy is for us as far as our spiritual lives go, reconciling Singleton sexuality and spirituality is not exactly an easy endeavor (given that we are lacking help in the religion department). But we need to give it our best shot, since I doubt that Inner Poise would be a goal worth seeking if it also required us to become asexual for the better part of our lives (nor is it acceptable to continue separating our sense of spirituality from our sexual experiences).

Shagging and Snogging *Can* Be Divine (but it's up to us to make it that way)

~

As a beginning response to the above questions, I will say that most of us who have had our share of shagging experiences, à la Miss Jones, know by now that it's not as if having lots of sex *really* lands us in a spiritual Mecca; nor does it land us in an endless, meaningless void either. Sex is many things for us: it can be at once painful and wonderful, a tremendous risk and giving of self, a mistake or an amazing realization of love. We are girls who are enlightened enough to know that, though the shagging lives of Becky and Bridget go off with nary a hitch (aside from a pregnancy scare or two), that the reality of our own sex lives, while thrilling, can also be disappointing and more complicated than these novels reveal. (Though I will add here that the extensive discussions among Bridget and friends about the emotional "immaturity" of bosses like Daniel can make sex, though fun at the time, lacking in meaning after the fact and not the best experience from which to unite our spiritual and sexual selves.) As the audience of Chick Lit, we are also old enough to know that there's no *one* way to go about expressing ourselves as sexual beings either; we "make our own beds" on this issue. For some of us, no sex *is* still the best sex of all, and waiting until we find a soul mate is the appropriate way to fulfill our desires (though must admit, feel as if this is a dying breed of women). For others (dare I say most of us), waiting until Smug Marriage finds its way into our life (again, if it does at all) to have sex is simply not an option; we are not about to wait. So in support of the spiritual, Singleton shag, here are my suggestions.

Suggestion Number One

Despite the rather across-the-board idealization of marriage as the only acceptable receptacle for sex (am rhyming), surprisingly, somewhere within the vast majority of spiritual traditions across the world there are heavy streaks of eroticism (take, for example, the *Kama Sutra*). Desire for God expressed metaphorically through the language of human sexuality, kissing, touching (and all that good stuff) is actually celebrated in one of the most famous books in Hebrew scripture (which is also Christian scripture): *The Song of Songs*. *The Song of Songs* is as sexual a poem as you can find, and the fact that it is considered a sacred text is a step in the right direction as far as sexuality and spirituality goes. Though while there is a positive kernel in the erotic expression of divine desire, it only gets us so far, since spiritual traditions that use erotic language and ecstasy to describe divine love do so metaphorically (the metaphor part being especially important for religious folk here). But my advice is to take this seed of the erotic and *not* read it as merely metaphorical, and instead allow it to help us see the spiritual side of sexuality, regardless of whether we are Smug Married or not (I'll talk about the erotic, romantic side of the spiritual in Chapter Ten).

Suggestion Number Two

In an interview with *The Believer,* scholar Elaine Pagels (recently in the news constantly due to *The DaVinci Code* craze) discusses the etymology of the word *authority*. She mentions authority because of a turn in conversation about how so many people today are "disenchanted" with religious authority, since the sets of rules we continue to be given do not seem to add up with our lived experiences. (For example— and this is my example not Dr. Pagels's: we experience that sex can be good, as in virtuously good, even if when we are not married.) Pagels explains that the word *authority* "comes from the Greek word, *autours,* which means 'self.'" Regarding the claims of religious authority, she argues that, "Basically one has to go back and verify for oneself what authority one is going to accept." The way in which we experience authority and allow authority to direct our beliefs and actions ultimately rests within us: it is within us to decide *whose* authority is valid and where the moral rules that govern our lives and sense of self come from (v. promising idea).

Elaine Pagels's reminder to us of the origins of authority as a concept and the fact that it is historically rooted within the self is helpful as we try to reconcile spirituality and shagging, Singleton style. Seeking Inner Poise with regard to sex *should* involve remembering the following: that regardless of the choices we make about sexuality, none of these choices need alienate us from the spiritual life. We don't have to keep our sexuality and our spirituality separate; it's just that we are made to think unmarried sex and religion are incompatible. Ultimately, it rests within us to understand our sexual experiences as *either* valuable to our spiritual journeys *or* as hopelessly selfish and vacant of love, as Christopher West suggests. We have the authority (if we choose to take it) to read *The Song of Songs* as metaphorical *or* as a sacred poem that helps us see the spiritual side of our sexual experiences, if indeed we experience sex as meaningful, poetic, romantic, and loving in the same way that this beautiful poem portrays it.

Suggestion Number Three (and finally)

While it is empowering to realize that the authority to accept or reject certain rules or moral imperatives lies within us, we must temper our sense of authority by remembering that

Inner Poise is not a solitary affair, in the same way that our experience of sexuality encompasses another person. In thinking about the power we have to enfold the spiritual into the sexual, we should remind ourselves that the process of discovering the spiritual dimensions of our sexuality is a communal affair, even if the community consists only of two. Ultimately, it takes the authority and willingness of both persons to affirm the spiritual significance of sexuality. Who our partner is and the nature of the relationship we have with that person will influence the degree to which we can draw spirituality into our sexual experiences, or whether any degree at all is possible (as experiences that are one-night shags and sex with emotionally deficient partners are probably not good candidates for discovering the spiritual side of shagging). As we think about the spiritual side of sex, we must also think about the parameters in which we are experiencing it: sex in a loving relationship will obviously have more spiritual significance than sex with someone we barely know at all. It's the difference between Bridget's wild yet ultimately unsatisfying shagging relationship with Daniel (as she does not love him, just lusts him rather badly) and her experiences with Mark Darcy, a man who loves her deeply and with whom she has a much better chance of becoming the irresistible sex goddess she would like to be.

To conclude here on this most important topic for us: the thinking that we need to divorce our spiritual identities from our sex lives until we are married is a perspective that *we* have the authority to change *as a generation* (both men and women, straight and gay). Those of us who've experienced the ups and downs of Singleton sex should be confi-

dent that, despite the complications that sexuality presents
within relationships (any relationships for that matter, including Smug Married ones), sex ultimately *can be* a way to
celebrate and love the body, both our own and that of another (who perhaps has the body of Colin Firth which, I
think, would probably be easy for most of us to love if the
opportunity arose!). Learning to have authority over our sexuality is a subversive act; it takes away the taboos and pre-
scriptions we learn from religious authority and allows
sexuality to become an important part of our spiritual journeys and growth in relationships. Inner Poise, when it comes
to sexuality, truly starts within us, as it is up to us and our
partners to discover the sacred nature of our sexuality, *regardless* of whether we experience sex as Smug Marrieds or
Singletons. (Insert Ms. Jones's sigh of relief here, that Inner
Poise, reaching spiritual epiphany, *and* shagging Mark Darcy
can all exist happily together if she just lets them.)

6

"Up the Fireman's Pole"
Career as Spiritually Liberating or Bane of Existence?

*Badly behaved men in powerful positions: many (v. unfortu-
nate). Annoying colleagues: also many (why must everyone
be so gossipy?). Affairs with bosses conducted by Bridget: 1
(v.g., as 1 out of 3 respectable ratio). Number of Bridget's
resignations: 2 (grrrrr—but was begged to return on both
counts. Ha!).*

What's a Girl Like You Doing in a Males-Only Place Like This?

~

"What are doing here young lady?"

A grey-haired man complete with pot belly (like the
pig) and requisite suit waddled up and asked me this at a
conference not too long ago.

"Same thing you're doing here grandpa," I think to
myself but do *not* utter out loud, as calling the chair of a well-
known department in my field at a high-ranking university
"grandpa" is not good for future career prospects.

"And," I muttered silently to myself, "what do you

mean, *young lady?* What's that supposed to mean? Don't patronize me, you anachronistic patriarchal relic!"

Next I remind myself (again silently), "Oh *of course* you are patronizing me! My whole profession is built on patriarchy! How could I forget? I'm in the business of *religion,* where grey-haired old men like you are a dime a dozen."

While jutting my hip, flicking my hair in dramatic fashion, and batting my eyelashes for the purpose of emphasizing the feminine wiles that render me so obviously out of place in the field of religion, I respond out loud: "I was invited to give a presentation on the book I am currently working on." I say this, of course, in my sweetest, most innocent demeanor. I study his nametag and then add, "I'm speaking just before your presentation, actually, and I must go prepare. Bye-bye now!"

I add a sweet "yes grandpa" smile, and before he can say anything more, I turn gracefully on my stiletto heels and walk away in manner of model on catwalk in full hip-swing. Nothing like showing off all the reasons that make me a contradiction in terms in my chosen profession.

"Grrrrr!" I think, as my heels make loud, satisfying clicks on the cobblestones. Will there *always* be men to not take me seriously? *Must* I start dressing like a nun (which in my career would not be out of the question) to stop people from raising eyebrows and inquiring as to whether or not I am "here with my mum?" or whether I mind telling how old I am? Hmmm?

If the authors of Chick novels could answer my questions, I think they would respond with a resounding, "Yes! This is what the world of work is like for women."

Pass the Inner Poise please . . .

Message Jones: You Appear to Have Forgotten Your Skirt (Oops!)

~

Between Daniel Cleaver and Richard Finch, Bridget has her own share of naughty supervisors in need of conversations with HR about bad behavior (in other words, how *not* to get the company sued). Throw Mr. Titspervert into the mix—a man who prefers to converse with the chests of female employees as if they have no heads—and we get quite the devilish Trinity. Although, let's be honest and acknowledge that Bridget's many minutes spent lusting after Daniel don't exactly help her realize that his instant messaging about sick skirts and see-through tops is thoroughly inappropriate. Instead of seeing warning signs, Bridget learns the hard way that cultivating a relationship with the person above you at work does not *literally* translate to shagging him. (Though if Hugh Grant were playing the part of our boss, it might indeed be difficult to maintain professional office behavior and be totally understandable to shag him once or twice by accident.) While adventures with Mr. Cleaver leave Bridget breathless for a time, when he chucks her for a "bronzed giantess" from America, her experience at the office turns so unbearable she quits. To make matters worse, Bridget faces a steady stream of complaints from Mum and Una Alconbury that careers today are making women totally unmarriageable (excellent).

Work for Bridget is a *struggle,* as it is for many of us. We want so much to get it right, to find our ideal calling and fulfillment in what we do. We pray that *just this once* the honeymoon period at our new job survives longer than a couple of weeks. But as honeymoons always seem destined to end, practically minutes after Bridget triumphantly trades Daniel and publishing for television, she ends up in the clutches of mildly psychotic Richard Finch, whose intentions involve humiliating her in front of millions to raise ratings (though at least there is no danger of Bridget shagging *him*). A dirty old man obsessed with sex, Finch wants nothing more than to dress his female reporters in teensy skirts and place them in compromising situations. Bridget does experience one major con-

It is central to our spiritual growth that our work experience not resemble being tortured as if we are captured CIA agents with information for which another government would like to pull our teeth.

solation in the career department, however, when *Sit Up Britain* acknowledges that they simply can't do without her, and what looks to be a successful career in television reporting is in her future. (And on top of being told she is needed, Finch gets the sack!) The fantasy we all long for finally becomes Bridget's reality—to suddenly hear our supervisors utter those words: "We simply can *not* do without you!"

Fellow heroines Becky Bloomwood (*Shopaholic*), Melissa Fuller (*Boy Next Door*), and Kate Reddy (*I Don't Know How She Does It*) face similar difficulties in their own career aspirations. Becky struggles because no one ever takes her seriously, dealing with constant humiliation and lack of confidence in her ability to succeed as a financial reporter. The evilness of bosses, gossipy employees, and the Big

Brother–like machine of Human Resources features prominently in all of Meg Cabot's books. Cabot's heroines are constantly receiving hilarious admonishments from the higher-ups or other HR persons in the form of passively aggressive e-mails and letters. (But the upside for Cabot's *Boy Next Door* and *Boy Meets Girl* is that Cabot approaches the workplace with a "what goes around comes around" mentality in manner of Karma, both good and bad, so readers can always feel confident that all evil work demons will get their due in the end.) For financial wizard Kate Reddy to maintain what has been hard-won success managing Hedge Funds (hmmm: Hedge Funds? Perhaps related to Hedge Hogs?), she has to become the uber-Mom, with nary a second to find some inner peace of her own, not to mention constantly smiling with gritted teeth as disgustingly chauvinistic men at the office evaluate her bra size and comment on her legs.

This is all rather depressing isn't it?

Gaaahh! Work as Endless Treadmill (without thigh-slimming benefit)

~

Pursuing a career was supposed to change *everything* for women, or so women thought back in the 1960s and 70s. By leaving the house and getting a job, we would finally find ourselves on equal footing in society with men, at once satisfying our urge for something more than housewifery, while at the same time enjoying the independence and freedom gained through education and buying power (buying power: yummy). For thousands of years, women have faced religion and patriarchy in collusion in the career department—The Man fighting to keep the woman behind closed doors suckling the kids, all in the name of the equally Manly Christian trifecta-God, Allah, YHWH (or whichever other divinity happened to be around). The only real career available to women other than wife and mother involved giving up sex for life and becoming a nun (if you were or are Buddhist or Christian) and, eventually, later on in history (according to my mother), becoming a teacher or nurse. But at long last (at least in the West), women broke free of the double grip, defying both societal and religious patriarchy and pursuing our passions through the job market and public life as men have done for ages, yet in manner as if we are men ourselves (hurrah?).

How did we get here exactly? Why is it that navigating the workplace seems akin to passing through a minefield for today's working girl? Well for one, while the malingering influence of the male-dominated workforce is quite prominent for many of us, another problem we face is that corporate and institutional cultures don't make allowances for the fact that we don't have wives at home taking care of our kids and preparing meals for us daily. We are often expected to commit our entire souls to the organization at the expense of everything else in our lives (in manner of poor Kate Reddy). Even though today women account for a massive percentage of the workforce, we still find ourselves in positions where we must conform to workplaces designed for, by, and to accommodate men. We arrive at work to find frat boys with most of the power and prestige, expecting us to "heh-heh-heh" after their not-so-funny jokes, all the while overlooking their incompetence and inappropriate behavior while expressing our deep inner need to play golf and smoke cigars.

(Feel endless desire, even intense *need* to name real-life examples of incompetent supervisors here, yet will refrain for
fear of lawsuit. In fantasy world I insert full names and job
affiliations here in manner of payback. Hmmm. Am having
fantasy now.) Rather than being inspired to greater creativity and self-nurturing, we are told to pay our dues and keep
quiet about unfair practices because "that's just how things
work here," maneuver dysfunctional systems, and pander to
the chain of command. (OK, comment might be teeny anecdote from personal experience.) We are often faced with two
choices: to remain obedient to the way things are or risk our
positions. The formula is very simple: first pay your dues,
then you can do things differently if you want. (V. unfortunate that dues-paying generally does not come with the
fringe benefit of belonging to swanky NYC-style club like the
one in SOHO that Samantha from *Sex* so desperately wanted
membership to one summer.)

 Whether we have bosses like Melissa's or Becky's,
who refuse to recognize our potential, or psychotic supervisors as Bridget does, the workplace does not seem exactly
ideal for spiritual growth. In fact, theologian Dorothee Soelle
compares the type of work experience described by our heroines to being stuck on an endless treadmill. (As if walking the
treadmill *after* leaving the office is not enough!) Like Sisyphus,
the mythical man doomed to a life of pushing a boulder up
a mountain, only to watch it roll back down so he can repeat
the process, the workplace evokes a similar encounter for us.
For Soelle, the day-in, day-out grind of the alarm ringing, drag-
ging ourselves to what is often a less-than-uplifting office en-

vironment, pushing ourselves through the day to make it to leaving time is a metaphorical treadmill. To make matters worse, she informs us that the treadmill of work that we so dutifully subject ourselves to during the day and afterward (as taming thighs' desire to expand uncontrollably is high priority) was originally conceived as a torture device. I repeat to let this shocking news sink in: a torture device! Treadmills were once used to torture people! Thus remaining in dysfunctional work environments like the ones we laugh and cringe about in *Shopaholic,* with Bridget, and certainly with supermum Kate Reddy, is akin to subjecting ourselves to torture! (Though must admit, can easily imagine Bridget screaming out to evil boss Daniel, "Torture me! Torture me! I will walk the treadmill endlessly if I must," which of course translates to "Shag me! Shag me please, you naughty, naughty boss!")

To be creative does not mean we all need to become artists. It means that we must be given the space to contribute positively and with a degree of autonomy at our jobs.

Why, oh why, can't we all be like Carrie Bradshaw? The only treadmill her feet seem to hit is the NYC sidewalk and in the cutest of shoes, *of course.* Her career leads her sexy self to adorn city buses; she seems to have a mostly invisible boss and an overall lack of sexism in her career, and her work allows her to be creative, shop without guilt, and lunch with friends on a daily basis. While she may struggle regarding men in her love life, she seems relatively free from

The Man when it comes to her work. Thinking about our lucky Carrie may lead some of us to shout, in manner of the Kates, Beckys, and Melissas of the world: "Stop! I want to get off this ride! I want a healthy career that inspires my creativity, motivates me to aspire to great things, and does not suck all the remaining energy I have! I want shopping not golf!" Fear not. Like our funny female protagonists, we may be somewhat lacking in the power and autonomy department as far as work goes, but there's still spiritual possibility to be found on the job market (with a little work of course—hee-hee).

Spiritual Environmentalism at the Office (Hmmm. Feng shui?)

~

Despite the leering frat boys, the politicking in the office, the nagging HR always reminding us that "we can be replaced," and that unfortunate torture-treadmill situation, our experience of work *can* and *should* be pivotal to our spiritual journey. For Soelle, it is central to our spiritual growth that our work experience not resemble being tortured as if we are captured CIA agents with information for which another government would like to pull our teeth. (Unless, of course, the CIA torture scenario involves playing the role of sexy double agent Sidney Bristow channeled by Jennifer Garner on *Alias*. Then teeth-pulling is fictional event all in manner of a typical day of work as Hollywood starlet.) In fact, Soelle claims that, "Good work releases the divine element in us." When many of us spend more than half (half!) our waking hours in the workplace, with colleagues and managers as our primary companions, it is easy to realize why work *should* be central to spiritual growth and also clear why we must figure out how to make work a more uplifting experience in the spirituality department—a valuable resource that helps us discover the divine, as Soelle suggests it can.

According to Soelle, for work to contribute to our spiritual growth, it must have three magical ingredients (note: must become like Hermione at Hogwarts). Number one: the workplace should be an environment that welcomes self-expression. As the divine is associated with creativity, so we must be able to see ourselves as part of the creative process in what we do. To be creative does not mean we all need to become artists. It means that we must be given the space to contribute positively and with a degree of autonomy at our jobs. Micro-management, the suffocation of new ideas, sexism on the job, reminders of where one "fits" in a hierarchy are all things that stifle self-expression.

In many ways, the work life of Carrie Bradshaw represents the epitome of self-expression as Soelle imagines it. Carrie's job is essentially a creative-writing position, where whatever question, idea, or reflection she has she turns into her column. While the column and the paper provide certain parameters for her work, she retains a great expanse of freedom of movement in what she chooses to write about. And the writing life leaves her open not only to personal creativity but to a freedom-filled lifestyle that few of us ever enjoy.

Which brings us to number two on Soelle's list of factors inspiring spiritual growth: the workplace must be an environment that fosters social-relatedness and a sense of community (but generally not in manner of shagging the boss). Rather than *discouraging* relationships by creating a rigid chain of command, diminishing the possibility of professional relationships due to uncomfortable sexist behavior, or facing the ever-present sense that "we can be replaced," the workplace should, ideally, cultivate a sense of our meaningful place in a larger whole. A work environment that tells us our job is in constant peril—the kind of peril that Kate Reddy constantly faces in her efforts to "balance" family and career—an office that requires allegiance to the boss above family and friends is not a healthy place to be, either professionally or personally. When Cannie Shapiro (*Good in Bed*) faces a personal crisis that challenges her professional life, rather than send her packing, the *Philadelphia Examiner* adjusts to support her new life situation to *keep* her: her colleagues actually care about her and what she contributes. In other words, they cringe at the idea of losing her. A job that makes us feel needed, that evokes a sense of solidarity with fellow employees rather than cut-throat competition, and that supports the ideal that *all* relationships are important and not just for political purposes (including those outside our professional life), is a workplace set up to promote spiritual growth.

The third and final ingredient for spiritual promotion at work is that it should connect us to the environment (nature). On this point, Soelle may be a *bit* outdoorsy for the likes of Bridget and Carrie, but I think we can interpret her view on this subject in a way that works for us city girls, too.

(Don't get scared! Spiritual work will not require us to go camping or exchange heels for Birkenstocks, I promise.) For Soelle, we are all participants in creation—*creation* here meaning the global community, the environment that is the natural earth, and the larger world that includes many nations and peoples, rich, poor, peaceful, and war-torn. In an ideal world (literally) our work should help us to hear the "groaning of creation," urging us to do what we can to right the injustices that our larger world community faces on so many levels. Our heroines, at least in the way that Soelle suggests, are in need of some serious self-evaluation on the relationship between their work and the world (as are many of us). Aside from teenage princess extraordinaire Mia Thermopolis, who expresses an acute desire to change the world beyond her doorstep, the working dreams of our Chick heroines are largely insular and restricted to their immediate communities, and they could stand to learn a lot from Mia. Ultimately though, Soelle is concerned about the relationship between work, justice, and spiritual transformation, and although it may be worth our while to do some thinking about where we are in this area, we should also remind ourselves that sometimes the little things we do, in manner of reconciling work with being a good neighbor (Melissa Fuller) or righting an unjust termination of an employee (Kate Mackenzie), are at least a good beginning. (Though must admit that getting down and dirty with the earth will never be this girl's calling, no matter how spiritually grown I hope to become, so perhaps rearranging office environment to maximize feng shui experience will have to do!)

Becoming a Visionary at Work:
A Woman Needs a Fantasy

~

When I finish novels like *I Don't Know How She Does It* and *Good in Bed,* there is a part of me that wants to celebrate their protagonists for figuring out a way to pursue a career and find a fulfilling life outside the office altogether, and there is a part of me that wants to cry, too. I am cheering that Kate Reddy finds a route to success, however bumpy, but somewhere deep within I am also angry at her for not *changing things*— for not showing how a woman can hang on and make things better in the office space that most of us occupy and will forever occupy because that is our lot. But when I feel the flash of dismay and anger, it quickly turns to forgiveness of both heroine and author, because then I remind myself that it is my generation's fantasy that the workplace will magically change on our watch or, even better, that it will disappear altogether from our lives.

These novels, however funny, are both a biting critique of a woman's experience of the workplace *and* a fulfillment of our secret fantasy to *find a way out,* to discover and realize our own inner Carrie Bradshaw with her excessive amount of free time and an ideal circumstance in which to realize all of her many questions, ideas, and reflections. The goals of the Bridgets and Beckys seem to involve somehow getting out from under The Man: finding their big break, selling that screenplay, getting a spot on television, doing whatever it takes so that they can be free agents of a sort. In other words, their work life in many cases is resolved by *leaving.* Or if not forgoing the workplace altogether, they strive to become the boss—or at least one of the bosses at the office, replacing a less friendly overlord in the process (as in both Meg Cabot's *Boy Next Door* and *Boy Meets Girl*). Either way, what we see happening with our heroines is a shift in the center of power: power goes from being outside our heroines' control to being centered within them.

In spite of the many struggles these women face in the workplace, they eventually all seem to find themselves in positions where they feel needed, where someone has recognized their potential, their intelligence, and their creativity. We are thrilled when Bridget finds the chutzpah to walk out on evil boss Daniel, leaving his jaw hanging. We applaud Cannie for getting that screenplay sold while at the same time handling pregnancy and motherhood. And we love that Becky Bloomwood not only publishes a front-page article but then lands a spot on a talk show. (Not to mention the fact that she lands her big break by trying to right a genuine wrong simply because it *is* wrong, not because she wants fame and fortune, though the fact they are a byproduct doesn't hurt!) We want to see these women triumph in their work, their wildest hopes and dreams realized, in the same way we hope to find this in our own lives. We want them to find success in a way

> The women authors of Chick Lit are visionaries of a sort—contemporary women mystics who have given us subversive models for Girlhood, all while tickling our funny bones and reaching our hearts.

that makes The Man's jaw drop, as they walk away from dysfunctional environments. It is in exploring these possibilities—fantasies of a sort (even if only in our heads) in telling the boss off (even if only in fiction)—that we explore other avenues and possibilities of fulfillment and how things could be different for all of us.

A long time ago, in a galaxy far, far away, becoming a visionary—a spiritual one, as in having visions of the divine—used to give women a lot of authority in the workplace and public affairs. In fact, claiming to have special, spiritual knowledge or visions gave women a lot of power, so much that some women, like medieval mystic Catherine of Siena, had enough authority to give the Pope (the pope!) a piece of her mind, when she wanted to, about his political dealings. A woman mystic's ability to see God, literally in the form of visions, gave her the power to teach and to preach, to write, and to speak on matters spiritual in ways usually reserved for men only. Being a visionary at work got women promoted in a rather grand sort of way, as it gave them the kind of power in society usually reserved only for men at this time in history.

In many ways, but especially in light of women's visionary history, we can claim that the spiritual life requires quite the active imagination as far as work goes. In *Mysticism and Vocation,* James Horne describes the discovery of one's calling as mystical in nature, claiming that in some cases a "person decides to undertake important projects or missions, or even their vocation in life, in the midst of the mystical process." He explains "mystical illumination" as a "central visionary experience . . . that results in the resolution of a personal or religious problem." Mystical visions, for Horne, help us visualize how things could be different, better, more purpose-filled and fulfilling. In a similar vein, in *Becoming Divine* Grace Jantzen discusses the importance of a woman's ability to project (or fantasize) her deepest desires in her endeavors to become spiritually fulfilled. "Projections need to be those which embody our best and deepest aspirations, so we are drawn forward to realize them." For Jantzen, our ability to visualize or project and endeavor to fulfill these hopes and desires is related to our ability to see the divine operating within our efforts.

With regard to career, in many ways women today *have* to begin with the fantasy, because the reality is not quite as pretty as Carrie's shoe collection and more resembling of Soelle's torturous treadmill. But having an active fantasy life, for Jantzen, is not so different from becoming a mystic: it requires our ability to see the divine, or at least the possibility of the divine, on the horizon in even the most unlikely of circumstances. The women authors of Chick Lit, by exposing the realities of what so many women face and then giving us heroines who hang on to their dreams and forge their own paths, in many ways are like the women mystics who left what was the traditional path for the woman in their day— the home and motherhood—for a place where autonomy, self-expression, and meaningful relationship became possible in new ways. As real-life women (though we may wish to be the fictional characters we adore), we *are* where we *are* in our own work experiences. But we can also put stock in the fact that indulging in fantasy is a mystical activity; it stays with us in a way that it can change our future if we let it. When we see what's on the other side of the cubicle, we can't help but try and get there somehow.

I have no doubt that the women authors of Chick Lit are visionaries of a sort—contemporary women mystics who have given us subversive models for Girlhood, all while tickling our funny bones and reaching our hearts. They are women who've made it, just like their characters: they've gotten out of the rat race and found careers that are rooted in self-expression and meaningful relationship (and lacking in grey-haired male figures who insist on calling them "young lady" in manner of the v. condescending). They find a space in the world of work where they can thrive and grow. The message from the women authors of Chick Lit seems to be that if we listen to what our hearts tell us, if we are true to ourselves, if we do what we know is right, *if we dare to imagine what could be,* then things will work out for us in the long run. If we have faith in where our passions lead us, then the kind of success that leads to fulfillment in the work department is in our future. And while we may not sell a screenplay just in the nick of time in manner of Cannie Shapiro, we can still find hope in the triumphs of these women that, in the end, it's through being a *visionary* of sorts that they all save themselves.

7

Bread and Wine Among Friends
Finding Spiritual Community at a Local Bar

Members in Church of Bridget: 1 (Bridget). Alcohol units for sacramental sharing: limitless (as alcohol consumed in ritualistic, communion-like behavior totally excusable). Available bread for breaking: none (but have chocolates lying around so will use in lieu of wafer as chocolate practically sacred anyway).

Worshipping at the Church of Bridget
(minus the churchgoing part)

~

Aside from celebrating the Christmas holiday, showing up in church for weddings, and sending her to Sunday school for a few years, Bridget's family hasn't done much to instill religious sensibility in her (as Mummy seems too frivolous for religion anyway). As a Singleton, it is free-form friendship rather than family or religion that is Bridget's sustaining force and provider of nurturing community. When she needs a good laugh, a shoulder, a rant, or a post-shagging celebration discussion, she calls on Jude, Sharon, and Tom, as they call on her whenever the need for togetherness arises. These four are a makeshift family of their own, relying on each other for both emotional and social support. If one amongst them goes missing (for instance, the ever-sarcastic-yet-lovable Tom), the communal binding forces kick into high gear, and a mission to find and rescue he-who-has-gone-astray ensues (who turns out to be hiding in flat due to a few nose alterations of the plastic surgery variety). If a member of the tribe needs moral support (namely, Bridget), her friends are more than willing to be there for her with an abundance of unconditional love and a blind eye, as we saw in the first Bridget movie: a post-Bridget-cooking disaster on her birthday.

"We get by with a little help from our friends" is the prevailing theme among most novels of the Chick persuasion, not to mention the example set on the small screen by *Sex and the City*. What would Carrie, Samantha, Miranda, and Charlotte do without each other? When Carrie went off to Paris to be with artiste-luva (emphasis on the *luh*) Aleksandr, Charlotte, Miranda, and Samantha felt her absence acutely, their usual gatherings seeming infinitely smaller without her. It is friendship consecrated through lunches, happy hours, and shopping trips that defines their lives and heals their loneliest moments. When *Good in Bed*'s Cannie Shapiro finds herself in a tight spot, some assistance and an extended re-treat with devoted friend (and movie starlet) Maxi become her saving grace. In Elizabeth Young's *A Promising Man,* Harriet Grey would be lost without roomies who double as dear companions, helping her get over snippy gossip when it is aimed in her direction and recognize a good guy when he shows up at her doorstep. As we go out into the world, armed with our higher educations and career aspirations, our friends tend to become our surrogate families, providing all manner of assistance, be it money (because sometimes we get ourselves in a tight spot), self-esteem (when ours seems to be out on holiday), or just plain old love (despite the fact that we've served them horrible blue soup, as Renée Zellweger's Bridget does accidentally at her dinner party). By the time Singletons approach thirty and swiftly pass this landmark year, a shift in one's tight-knit group can feel painful and scary.

> *Like a Jewish seder or a Christian worship service, gathering together around a meal is one of the most tried-and-true ways in which to practice spiritual fellowship.*

Yet regardless of what are numerous, albeit humorous, tales of contemporary community formed between long-term Singletons, à la *Sex and the City* and Ms. Jones, we do not see a lot of prayer and other ritualistic activity going on in celebration of urban togetherness. It's notable that the stuff comprising sacred ritual and community *is* often present at assemblies: alcohol units abound (good if you are Christian), and multicourse dinners complete with candlelight are not uncommon (excellent if you are Jewish). But for all intents and purposes, these supportive, nurturing gatherings, held together by the glue of unconditional love, are decidedly secular (and most often occur at a bar or flat in lieu of, let's say, *a synagogue*). Of course, the absence of traditional religious celebration is not shocking. Can you imagine sex-goddess Samantha raising a designer Cosmo at Balthazar in manner of a priest raising a wine-filled chalice at the altar of a traditional church? Or Bridget, Tom, Shazzer, and Jude uttering a prayer of thanks before every meal (or glass of wine)?

Despite the starring role friendship plays in our lives, when it comes to spirituality we seem to vote for the Independent Party. In Bridget's life, she boldly charges toward Inner Poise, yet does so in manner of a rather sovereign goddess (at least on the surface); Bridget's spiritual pursuits happen more or less *apart* from her friendships. While she mentions her search and yearnings to Tom, Shazzer, and Jude at various points, overall they seem neither to impede nor inspire her interest in Inner Poise. It *is* true that Inner Poise for Bridget functions as a kind of ethical framework, helping her discern whether her actions are positively or negatively influencing her life and the lives of those around her. Yet the bulk of Bridget's *explicit* spiritual meanderings she shares with us only through her private diary. Hers is a largely inward journey, practiced in what I'll call the Church of Bridget—a church that seems not to require regular attendance or any other members for that matter (which in many ways is v. convenient, as can worship without leaving house). As we grow older and work hard to preserve our makeshift families in manner of Carrie, Samantha, Miranda, and Charlotte, I wonder whether membership in a spiritual community of only one is *the answer* to all of our prayers or instead a journey we will eventually find not only unsatisfying but too lonely and tragic to bear. (And as we all know, becoming spiritual epiphanied spinster is not v. good for achieving Inner Poise.)

Yikes! Am Spiritually Homeless!

~

For many of us, leaving behind organized religion and regular attendance at its weekly rituals is a huge relief. Structured religious practice has turned out to be a pain in the arse and empty of meaning for many of us, as it does not fit in with our busy lifestyle choices and beliefs. In my own experience, abandoning Catholicism (to be replaced by the more private Church of Donna, which, like the Church of Bridget, does not require leaving the house and have heard is also a v. fashionable community) has been cause for excited celebration rather than feelings of sadness and loss, and so far has contained not even an ounce of fiery brimstone-like repercussions. (Am keeping fingers crossed that gates of hell remain shut. Besides, running in fear from said gates simply not possible, as cute heels would obstruct sudden movement anyway.)

When my mother stopped forcing me to go to church in high school, my response was, "Hurrah! I'm no longer going to torture self in boring, endless, Sunday churchgoing! I'm now free to imbibe large amounts of coffee and read the paper in lieu of pursuing salvation of soul (excellent, as heaven seems v. remote location in manner of Siberia anyway)." I'm pretty sure Mom expected me to come back to the fold at some point, yet that particular point has not yet arrived.

Relief à la relinquishment of religious ritual (am alliterating now) has not always been the prevailing feeling historically, however. In *The Body and Society,* Peter Brown describes the disappointed reaction of an early convert group of Christians when leader Paul (this is *the* Paul who got struck by lightning and fell off his horse in the New Testament) rejected their proposal to practice perpetual virginity as a community. (All of them wanted virginity: men, women, children, elderly. Everybody. Shagging absolutely prohibited.) Paul explains in 1 Corinthians that the life of a virgin is destined only for the few *chosen* (like himself, for example). Smug Marriage (OK, he didn't really say Smug Marriage, just marriage) is reserved for everyone else, as most people are too weakened by human, lustful ways (since most of us are like Bridget). You'd think all of Corinth would be breathing a sigh of relief at this announcement, that they'd be thinking, "Whew, sex is still kosher—let's go out and celebrate with some good Smug Married shagging," right? Well, according to Brown, they were rather frustrated with Paul's rejection on this issue. Unlike the Jews with their laws, kosher eating habits, strict marriage codes, and annual Passover rituals—all of which marked them as a separate people—Christians seemed to blend in with every other pagan around. The Corinthians *wanted* to stand out as a group, united through shared ritual, much like the Israelites did. Without it, they felt "ritually invisible" or a kind of "spiritual homelessness."

One of the major and rather unfortunate repercussions of leaving organized religion behind (despite its many positive aspects) is that we lose the *organized part*. Of course, it is that pesky organized dimension that often makes us *want* to unburden ourselves from going through the ritual motions, because it's the organization that sets up what are seemingly impossible moral expectations for many of us. Most religious practices were designed to fit the lifestyles and concerns of people thousands of years ago (like the Corinthians for example), and institutionalized religion seems determined to hang on for dear life to unforgiving moral codes (especially with regard to sexual orientation and shagging), not to mention a view of women that's better suited for the Dark Ages. Though there were once practical reasons for kosher laws (maintaining a person's health), and it was once common to marry as early as age twelve, today these ritual holdouts have passed their sell-by date. Practices like "waiting until marriage" (for shagging) are dying out, and, as many of us have decades of Singleton life ahead of us, they are simply impractical. So goodbye glaringly sinful self—hello invisible purity! (Though possible negative repercussion would be inability to attract cute guy, for example, if one were invisible. Hmmm.)

SWF Seeking FSC (Singleton Wisecracking Female Seeking Friendly Spiritual Community)

~

You might be wondering why it matters at all whether our Bridget-esque and *Sex and the City*–style "congregations" formally consecrate a meal or enact some kind of ritualistic ceremony as part of gathering together. Or perhaps you are wondering whether, with a designer martini in one hand and sumptuous goodies in the other, we *are* in fact enacting something sacred? Or why we should even go about trying to reconcile martinis with mass anyway? Besides, people today don't want to impose their god on anybody else's god (as v. unbecoming behavior, much like setting up house right in the middle of someone else's flat without first asking permission or receiving invitation). Raise your martinis high, as spirituality without any of the bothersome religious ritual-moralistic part is liberating! I was just kidding about the downside of losing organized religion—right?

While taking control of our spiritual lives in manner of the v. independent can be liberating, I think we lose something more than just out-of-date moral expectations and too-early wake-up calls on the weekend when we give up on religion. Though the organization of traditional religious life can be quite alienating, it's also the organized part that provides the spiritual companionship. By losing the organization, there is no doubt that we gain freedom and control over our spiritual pursuits (v.g.), but with the freedom we lose the community, at least on a spiritual level (v. sad). In many ways, we twenty- and thirty-somethings are sort of damned if we do, damned if we don't when it comes to traditional religion and the communal ritual that accompanies it. We can get rid of the unhelpful, unforgiving expectations that feel about as comfortable as a five-inch pair of stilettos, but then we end up without a spiritual roof over our heads in a rather lonely Church of One.

> *Our challenge today is to anchor our personal journeys toward Inner Poise within the communities that already surround us, exploring the spiritual possibility in the rituals we already practice and the spiritual leaders we already are.*

Today Evangelical Christianity and Orthodox Judaism have practically become fads among twenty-somethings unsatisfied with all this spiritual wandering. Taking up a narrow interpretation of these traditions (one that tends to be very countercultural regarding sexuality and gender roles) has become popular among a generation looking for order and shared community in their lives. These young converts are not changing the messages in the tradition but instead are repackaging the ritual to fit a generation that has grown up on MTV and *The Simpsons* (as worship style often includes full-on garage bands as part of celebration, with Krispy Kreme donuts and Starbucks to follow. It's Homer Simpson's dream church). The major bonus of choosing this kind of path today is suddenly finding yourself in the open arms of a community, waiting with already-determined answers to all of life's questions, supported by a ritually filled life among fellow believers. Consecrated, ready-made community can be a welcome relief when someone starts to feel alone on the road to enlightenment.

While I find all of the above interesting (especially the Starbucks part), I am not about to become an Evangelical or an Orthodox Jew. I am also well aware that there are millions of career-oriented, shag-happy, independent women like Bridget who feel the same way (as we are filled with lust and like it that way). Though jumping on the more extreme end of the spiritual community bandwagon might not be the answer, opening ourselves up to the possibility of fellowship in our spiritual lives is something our generation needs to consider. If our friendship lives are as important as we make them out to be, and, if one of the reasons we faithfully watched *Sex and the City* (on Sundays no less) was how much we admired the strong female friendship of its characters, then perhaps worshipping at a Church of One requires some rethinking on our parts. After all, if in friendship we find ourselves amidst a community defined by unconditional love, support, laughter—not to mention adventure—then why leave spirituality, of all things, out? I happen to believe that it is *through* all of the above in our friendship communities that the spiritual significance of our lives becomes *most* obvious: our experiences together are the stuff of spiritual activity itself (Yessss!).

Yessss! Am Spiritual Leader! Was Lost But Now Am Found!

~

Did any of you *Sex and the City* fans who are reading this ever wonder whether the fact that it always aired on Sundays had any higher significance? It was practically Sunday mass for twenty- and thirty-something women (and some men, too), right? How many of you went to weekly gatherings on Sunday evenings that revolved entirely around sipping yummy drinks among girlfriends while seeing who Carrie and company shagged next? How many of you have ever attended a book club discussion, or even held your own, goodies included? How many of you reading this have ever called your friends together for brunch or a dinner party? Or spent hours over a meal at someone else's invitation? Though our makeshift gatherings in manner of *Sex and the City* and Bridget and company may not sound like obvious candidates for the next sacred thing, they provide an enormously rich place for us to see how spiritual community is already a part of our lives.

If we stop and think about it, we may call ourselves Singletons, but our lives are *filled* with the stuff of ritual and community (and experience that community over food and drink). Like a Jewish seder or a Christian worship service, gathering together around a meal is one of the most tried-and-true ways in which to practice spiritual fellowship, and we are no strangers to gathering around goodies. And while we're on the subject of food and fellowship, Ms. Jones practically has her own sacred holiday: the sacred feast day of the Celtic Goddess Brigid (that's right, there is a goddess *and* a saint by the name of Brigid). Each year on February first, in ancient Celtic culture (and still today in certain circles), worshippers gathered together to celebrate Brigid at a ritual called Imbolc. As Brigid is associated with spring, new life, and healing, this particular celebration was held to mark the coming of the spring season and renewal of the earth. The gathering traditionally has included dancing, feasting, and even (in ancient times) some ritual shagging (a feast Samantha *and* Bridget would surely love. Perhaps we all need to start celebrating Imbolc again every year—Huzzah!).

Sitting behind ritual in general, be it ancient or recent, are some pretty cool ideas. Ritual is designed to connect a believer to her community, to remind her of the ideals, beliefs, and morals that she has committed herself to, and to guide her in how to incorporate these things into her daily life, as the festival Imbolc is intended to remind us of rebirth.

Ritual is supposed to help us distinguish the sacred from the normalcy of life, to order our existence, our choices, our calendars, and sometimes even our homes. By participating in ritual, it's as if we have stepped onto a sacred plane, like stepping through a window that connects us to the god we have chosen to worship, and through that experience of the divine, we are connected to each other. Ritual is a kind of spiritual performance intended to transport us to a place where we can "commune" with the sacred, and within that place our lives, our beliefs, our relationships and practices are consecrated with and nurtured by the divine. (V. relevant question to ask here is whether spiritual performance can win us Oscar nominations so as to gain invitations to walk down red carpet in fancy, freebie gowns. But I will leave that for another conversation.) It is through *shared* ritual that our spiritual lives become connected to those we love, turning the conversations that occur over dinner into vehicles through which the sacred significance of our connections becomes apparent.

Growing up, most of us learn to associate spiritual leadership with the local pastor (if you are Christian), rabbi (if you are Jewish), or imam (if you are Muslim)—spiritual occupations for the few (mostly male) individuals who seek to take charge of the ritual side of religious life. Yet becoming a spiritual leader and overseeing "ritual performance" does not *have* to require leading large congregations in traditional forms of worship. In fact, spiritual leadership is far more common than we give ourselves credit for (or at least it can be if we let it). In *Preparing Spiritual Leaders: One Teacher Takes on the Challenge,* Judy Rogers talks about how

risky it feels for us to bring spirituality into the public dimensions of our lives; we have learned so well to tuck spirituality into the darkness of our private selves. For Rogers,
putting our spirituality on the line among others is a worthy,
even essential endeavor, especially if one is to become a
good leader and teacher of others. "We have to welcome
mind, body, heart, and soul into the learning process," and
barring spirituality from
public places only serves to
make it harder to integrate
spirituality into who we are
and what we do. While
Rogers risks drawing spirituality into her classroom
through the community she
forms with her students,
we face similar risks when
sharing our spiritual selves
among our families of
friends. Judy Rogers, though
not a minister or a rabbi, is a spiritual leader in her own right.
She is openly working to create space for shared spirituality
between herself and others—a task that makes her feel vulnerable but the rewards of which she feels immensely.

Spirituality isn't just about learning to love ourselves or a personal quest that happens in a vacuum. Without the experiencing of being loved and loving others, how would we know how to love ourselves in the first place?

　　　　Our challenge today is to anchor our personal journeys toward Inner Poise within the communities that *already*
surround us, exploring the spiritual possibility in the rituals
we *already* practice and the spiritual leaders we *already* are.
Embarking on a personal spiritual quest is one thing, but
learning to share that quest with others requires a willingness

to open our spiritual selves up to others, to bend and compromise to accommodate the needs and journeys of our friends in addition to our own, which calls for a vulnerability that isn't always easy. After all, it is easier to be a goddess alone than to be a goddess among many others (as too many divas in a single room can present problems).

Spirituality is meant to be shared and experienced with others; it has an other-centered component to it, as we all have an other-centered component to us. Inner Poise should not bring us simply an Inner Peace that we hoard to ourselves (in manner of hoarding celebration toffee). It is something that resides within us but that is also nourished by the love we feel from those around us and the loving that we do in response. After all, one of the most important things we learn from the experience of friendship is the need to show our friends that we love them and need them. Spirituality isn't just about learning to love ourselves or a personal quest that happens in a vacuum. Without the experiencing of being loved and loving others, how would we know how to love ourselves in the first place? Part of our journey toward discovering the goddess inside involves discovering the god/dess in everyone around us. As we call each other together over meals and beloved novels or for a night of shared *Sex and the City* or a yummy brunch, we are creating space in our lives where we can explore spiritual leadership and community in new ways. Through these "traditions," we open ourselves up to experiencing community and the connections we make with others through shared conversation and goodies as a divine activity in and of itself. After all, who says we can't celebrate the goddess over a Cosmo or two?

8

"Have You Noticed Anything Odd About Your Mother?"

Facing Family, Martyr Mums, and Smug Marital Obsessions on the Road to Enlightenment

Prayers uttered during family interactions: millions. Times Smug Marriage comes up in conversation with family: also millions. Guilt trips precipitated by Mummy's unsolicited commentaries: seemingly infinite. Desires for own future Mum-style Martyrdom: 0 (v.g. as prefer not to be thrown to lions in manner of ancient Roman traditions and instead watch lions on Discovery channel or at zoo).

Thank God for Grandmothers!

~

Any time I hear Lou Rawls on the radio, I can't help but think about my grandmother. There's nothing like his ultra-deep voice and all those bass keys on the piano to evoke her presence and our once-common joyrides in the block-long Lincoln Town Car that she loved so much (and occasionally knocked down our neighbor's mailboxes with).

"You'll never find . . . dum, dum, dum, dum, dum . . . another love like mine . . . dum, dum, dum, dum, dum," he would croon over her favorite radio station as we cruised along on another weekend journey to one of her beloved shopping malls (my grandmother was a goddess in the shopping department—I learned my skills from the best).

I had the fortune of growing up with my grandmother living in our house, quite the anomaly today given that many of us rarely see our elders' elders more than on the requisite holiday celebrations. As an only child, having Gram down at the other end of the house was quite a blessing: I had no siblings to share the burden of parental attention and the expectations placed on my future life and earnings. I learned quickly that when Mum said no, go to Dad, and when Dad said no, too, it was time to go to Grandma. All it usually took was a "Hey Gram, want to go shopping?" which inevitably elicited a "Sure, sweetheart," in response, and off we would go! Freedom!

Grandma's humming along to deep-voiced Lou ("Lady Love" was another of her favorites) while speeding along the highway in that boat of a car was like a sanctuary for me: family *without* all the guilt (and often a new purse thrown in or a yummy dinner).

God Help Me! When the Family Vacation Is Really a Guilt Trip

~

Unfortunately, Bridget seems without a fashionista-grandmum extraordinaire like mine to buffer her family's endless fixation on her life and need for Bridget to solve their various crises. If Bridget's mum and dad get themselves into a scrape (which seems to happen quite often), they ring Bridget, yet when she needs a talk and some advice, she certainly doesn't go ringing *them*. For a thirty-something, Bridget frequently interacts with Mummy, Daddy, and their large entourage of snippy relatives and friends, yet this is mainly due to the sheer force of Mummy's will and endless pestering phone calls rather than Bridget's own volition. Relatives and parental acquaintances seem more of a bother than anything else, and their role primarily involves harassing Bridget about whether or not she has snagged herself a permanent man and bothering her about having babies. Or *worse,* it takes the form of leering at her in manner of the v. disgusting, dirty old man, as with aging Geoffrey Alconbury, who never misses out on the opportunity to give Bridget a boyfriend-style hug (eeewww!) or squeeze her bottom (also, eeewww!). The elders in Bridget's life are not exactly providing her with supportive or desirable familial situations.

Family (the one that gave us life as opposed to the one we are supposed to acquire ASAP ourselves) seems a rather laughable minefield that heroines Bridget, Becky (*Shopaholic*), Cannie (*Good in Bed*), and Melissa (*Boy Next Door*) are left to navigate with only a thin film of patience to guide them. In the father department, while Bridget's daddy is sweet, he appears most of the time as a rather helpless tagalong on the roller-coaster ride that is Bridget's mum; he relies on his daughter for parenting instead of being a parent himself. Bridget's trauma in watching his helplessness is evident. While Becky Bloomwood's father plays the role of protective daddy, Cannie's is virtually absent altogether. When Cannie coincidentally runs into her father after years of distance, he leaves her painfully certain that she is a nonissue in his life. (I have yet to even mention Cannie's mum, who becomes a late-in-life lesbian and moves in with a woman twenty years her junior.) Melissa Fuller's father is mentioned only when she is e-mailing with Mom and generally under the auspices of, "Please don't tell Dad what's going on with me!"

So while fathers make appearances here and there in these stories, it seems that Mummy usually takes center stage as *the* primary tether to family for Bridget and friends. Mum is often the one who does the calling or the e-mailing, acting as official Minister of Information for all family interactions with offspring. Mummy is usually the person making sure we do not drop off the face of the earth when it comes to attending holiday celebrations and other familial obligatory contact. She is sometimes a woman who swoops in to rescue us in time of need, as when Bridget's mum gets her an interview, while at the same time filling the role of the woman who drives us to utter nuttiness by pestering us about all manner of things, mainly having to do with how we have somehow failed or disappointed her through merely going about our everyday lives (grrrrr). Whether we like it or not, Mum seems here to stay (sometimes rather literally when she shows up at flat unannounced).

And while we're on the subject of Mum . . .

The Martyr Mummy
(who really has her own agenda at heart)

~

Bridget's mum in particular has what Jennifer Baumgardner and Amy Richards would call the "Martyr Mom" complex (in manner of spiritual figure who gives up life, yet does not actually die). Martyr Moms are "passive-aggressive, making dinner for eight when they're exhausted, and then later hating you for it, essentially ceding their own lives in the thankless service of others." Sound familiar? She is the mum who is always reminding us how much she loves us, how much we are her *entire* life, but who in the next minute also notes how we will never, ever be truly grateful for all she has done (much like Mrs. Bennett from *Pride and Prejudice* who practically sees herself as queen Martyr Mummy).

Rather than being like a home that stays the same forever and for all generations to come, our experience of self is more akin to dwelling in a series of homes over the course of our lifetime.

Bridget's mum shows her martyr complex often, constantly uttering comments oozing with guilt-inducing implications. ("I'll be all right on my bloody own. I'll just clean the house like Germaine sodding Greer and the Invisible Woman.") At one point, Mum even implies that her children should feel guilty for her having given birth to them in the first place. She wears what Baumgardner and Richards describe as "self-denial like a blue ribbon." I really find it amazing how the guilt our mums can evoke in us is immediate and completely unrelenting, no matter how old we get (possibly God working through mums to punish us for our complete inadequacies in all areas of life).

In *I Don't Know How She Does It,* the fact that Kate Reddy is *not* a Martyr Mum evokes all sorts of disapproval from her in-laws. Unlike her sister-in-law Cheryl, who quit working as soon as she had her first child, Kate juggles career, Smug Marriage, and Mummyhood, paying for her choice with copious amounts of guilt. Due to this familial betrayal, Kate must endure not only comments from the in-laws that her husband Richard is looking awfully *thin* (translation: Kate! You are not taking care of our son like a woman should!) but subjection to her sister-in-law's perfect-wife-and-martyr-mum routine on holidays in addition. Kate is constantly faced with condescending remarks from Cheryl that on the surface sound innocent (sort of) but underneath communicate that Kate is not only an inadequate family woman but in the process is endangering her children as a result. In addition to breathing deeply, Kate manages the holidays, the in-laws, and Cheryl by reminding herself of the essential "spiritual" purpose Peter serves as husband to a martyr woman like Cheryl, musing that, "Peter plays the valuable role in Cheryl's life of the Cross I have to Bear. Every martyr needs a Peter, who, given time, can be trained up to not recognize his own underpants."

Martyrdom has certainly been a popular fad among women throughout the history of world religions; the vast majority of women expected *not* to cultivate any life or autonomy of their own for the sake of serving husband and children (at least until recently). Religion has generally designated the man as the breadwinner (you know, the hunter and gatherer), while the woman stays at home working day in and day out with no pay, making everyone happy but herself (just like Bridget's mum). The word *martyr* literally means "witness," and martyrdom as a lifestyle choice (if you can call it that) has held a place of esteem in religion, especially in Christianity.

Sometimes "bearing witness" requires the willingness to literally be willing to die for one's faith (in manner of being
thrown to the lions), but another way of understanding martyrdom includes extreme sacrifice *during* one's lifetime. The
traditional family has for centuries rested on the woman's willingness to sacrifice her own desires in a martyr-like fashion,
literally allowing husband and children to determine her life
(that, in the end, does not feel so fashionable).

The bitter taste of sacrifice is behind Bridget's mum's
passive-aggressive remarks about her own life choices, as
well as severe judgment about Kate Reddy's inadequacies by
her in-laws. Bridget's mother is a good example of the mum
who realizes what she has missed out on, yet somehow can't
resist pushing her daughter to follow the same footsteps, trying to force Bridget to focus herself on a man and babies
above all else (perhaps for the purposes of making Mum feel
better about her own life). It's as if many of our mums *know*
it wasn't ideal that they married at twenty (or nineteen or
eighteen) and had three kids by twenty-three, and *know* they
don't want us to do the same, but then somehow they need
us to understand the extent of their sacrifice (which, of course,
requires that we live their lives over again). Perhaps getting
to become a grandmother finally frees mums up to enjoy
children in a manner not previously possible.

Yet just as we long for our mothers to understand and
identify with the whys of our own decisions and different life
paths, I think that behind all their commentary and nagging
is a desire to be understood by us, too. According to Baumgardner and Richards, "For mothers, the challenge is to realize that their daughters came of age in an entirely different

era, one that makes their lives fundamentally different." It is not uncommon for mothers to be jealous of their daughters' lives and the freedoms they seem to take for granted. Given the ever-widening generation gap between us, a leap of faith seems to be in order on both ends to traverse the gulf in our lifestyles (but is never easy, especially when Mum's leaping abilities seem to be restricted to a willingness to leap into planning our weddings only and not to understanding daughter's needs and life aspirations). As we grow older, the pressure is more and more on us to do the leaping, and when leaping seems impossible, it is on us to be the ones to forgive and let go (though sometimes also v. forgivable on our parts to revert back to behavior with Mum as if still in secondary school and had never lived past thirteenth birthday).

Why the Obsession with Smug Marriage? Why? Why!

~

While we're discussing where, specifically, our mum is always ready to jump, a major familial theme that emerges among almost all our heroines is total obsession with what Melissa calls the M. word, which Bridget of course translates as Smug Marriage. (Though, I have to say that Cannie Shapiro may be the exception in this area, since her mother seems to be holding out hope that her daughter will forsake men altogether and discover her inner lesbian.) Aside from Cannie's mum pushing for lesbian love, much of the parental focus on the lives of their daughters can be summed up by the following questions:

1. Do you have a (Jewish/Hindu) Man yet?

2. If the answer is yes, is he a Marriageable (Jewish/ Hindu) Man?

3. If the answer is no, what are you doing to meet a Marriageable (Jewish/Hindu) Man?

4. Do you want us to set you up with our neighbor's son who is a Marriageable (Jewish/Hindu) Man (though balding and one foot shorter than you)?

5. If you cannot find a Hindu Man, would you like us to arrange your wedding to one who is also a doctor/ engineer?

My insertion of "Jewish/Hindu" in parenthesis prior to "Man" in questions 1–4 is for the benefit of my Singleton friends of Jewish and Indian descent, whose parents are often convinced that any Man who is not Jewish/Hindu (not to be confused with Jewish-Hindu) is also *never* Marriageable. And number 5 is really for the benefit of all my Indian girlfriends whose parents are willing to arrange their marriages at a moment's notice (but I suppose if you are Orthodox Jewish, arrangements may also be readily available to you too).

Between Bridget and others, family seems more of a comedy than a source of spiritual inspiration. But it is this nagging pressure from the parental units that late twenty- to thirty-something women need to settle down in manner of getting Smug Married, having children ASAP, and becoming their mums that is most evident and frustrating. The secondary debate that inevitably accompanies parental concern about

daughters finding Marriageable Men is whether or not shagging is a good idea prior to obtaining The One Ring To Rule
Them All (in manner of *Lord of the Rings*). Our mums seemingly feel the need to inform us, in various permutations, that
a woman should never give a man milk before he decides to
buy the whole cow. This loosely translates that wild premarital shagging will not obtain us the all-important diamond that
will make the man ours *forever* (not to mention protect us
from the gates of hell opening up and swallowing us in post-
shagging frenzy). The object of our lives as we approach
thirty and pass this landmark year is apparently landing a
(preferably) large rock on our left hand so our parents can
breathe a sigh of relief and, most of all, we can finally stop
robbing our mum of "the single joy [she] has left in life." The
single joy is Mum planning our wedding entirely on her own
without talking to us about any of the details first as if we are
eighteen and getting married rather than thirty-something
with ideas all our own.

The Traditional Family, Religious Identity, and Never-Ending Adolescence

~

Why the obsession with starting a family on the part of our
families in manner similar to Bridget's calorie counting? Why
the rush? Well, regardless of the separation of church and
state that we pretend to uphold in the West, we inherit and
often legally authorize our notion of family via religion. The
traditional family, according to both society *and* religion
across the world, usually consists of a man and woman united in marriage, plus their children (of course, traditional fam-

ily for the Muslim faith may include more than one wife, and I'm not even going to get into the whole Mormon polygamy issue). The essential component that "completes" a family in the eyes of most religions is not simply the marriage between man and woman but, more so even, it is about the couple's desire to procreate. The way the Catholic tradition has justified sex *within marriage* for thousands of years has been to excuse all the naughtiness as long as a couple is open to having children. Jewish identity is also centered on the family, not only in terms of worship within the home and education of children into the faith, but the survival and future of the Jewish people rests on one's children growing up, marrying another Jew, and having lots of offspring. Within Hinduism, if a woman today can't find a man (and finding a soccer hottie who is not also Indian doesn't suffice, as we saw in *Bend It Like Beckham*), parents are happy to arrange one, because what is a woman, after all, without a husband? In many Muslim countries, a woman isn't even allowed out of the house without a man, so what other choice does she have but to raise a family?

Just as we long for our mothers to understand and identify with the whys of our own decisions and different life paths . . . behind all their commentary and nagging is a desire to be understood by us, too.

In addition to the general support of the family structure by religious traditions, religions usually rely on family for the survival of the tradition itself. If families do not raise their children within a tradition and ensure that they grow up to start their own families, thus repeating the process, then the future of the religion is jeopardized. This is why religions like Christianity *fear* rising divorce rates, gays and lesbians, Singleton life, unmarried mothers, and basically any sort of lifestyle that departs from the traditional formula of growing up, getting married, having kids, and, ideally, raising them in a faith. And, God forbid (God is always forbidding it seems), a Catholic finally opts for Smug Married life but marries a non-Catholic or a Jew marries a non-Jew! Never mind the unspeakable horrors of a daughter committing herself to another woman, regardless of religious upbringing! Or that someone's child reaches her thirties without any Smug Marriageable prospects in sight! I must admit I couldn't help but snicker when I read recently in a Catholic magazine (I confess, as a professor I have to read this type of thing in addition to *Vogue* and *Elle,* though it's quite painful at times) that people of all faiths, including Muslims, Christians, and Jews, were banding together to protest the impending horrors of gay marriage becoming legal in the United States (of all things to tout as an "admirable" sign of interfaith unity).

Many of our parents lived their lives and constructed families governed by a traditional set of religious moral codes, regardless of whether or not they would consider themselves "practicing" in a tradition. While the families of our Chick heroines may not be super-religious, most of them *have* followed the traditional family formula. Cannie's nontraditional family is really a departure from the one with the mom, the dad, siblings, and perhaps a few other nutty relatives thrown in. In most families (except if we're Cannie), God forbid that we take the nontraditional route because we are

(1) gay or lesbian, (2) not interested in Smug Marriage, (3) more interested in our careers, (4) becoming a single mother, or (5) just not worried about family at the moment. If we choose any of the five options, inevitably our parents seem to freak out.

The fact that younger generations are finding the traditional family more difficult and sometimes less desirable to emulate, given cultural shifts, new opportunities (particularly for women) and attitudes toward sexual orientation, not to mention what psychologists have started calling the "emerging adulthood" phase in human development, this is more of a struggle for our elders than for us in the end. Instead of "settling down" at age eighteen like Mom and Dad, or even just after college, finding that IBM stability in the career department, having kids, and raising a proper family involved in the local church or synagogue, we are enjoying a highly extended "adolescent" period, bouncing around from significant other to significant other, job to job, flat to flat, in a way that makes our parents uneasy to say the least (not to mention the local priests and rabbis). Our parents want us to follow in their footsteps, and when we don't do things the way they did, it can make them uncomfortable, worried, and even angry. Sometimes this anger translates to thinking (especially the mums it seems) that we are purposely sabotaging our (which really means their) future happiness. As *our* sense of family shifts, in the same way that Bridget finds herself holding Daddy's hand through his crisis rather than the other way around, in many ways it is up to us to forgive our families as they try to understand our choices and forgive us for doing things a "little" differently.

Becoming a Spiritual Decorator at Home
(in manner of *Trading Spaces*!)

~

In *Good in Bed,* Cannie returns home one day to find that her
mother has packed up what was once her room, gotten rid
of her bed (of all things, the bed! Aaahhh!) to accommodate
Mummy's new lesbian lover's belongings, which include,
among other things, a loom. Needless to say, Cannie is rather
hurt and even angry at her mother's remodeling, especially
since she did so without asking Cannie first or even warning
her that it was going to happen. Most of us can relate to that
unsettling, upsetting feeling of someone touching—or worse,
rearranging—our stuff. At some point along the way, a roommate, a significant other, or our mothers have subjected us to
this experience, which often evokes a sense of insecurity; we
feel that we have somehow been violated. As creatures of
habit, we learn to make up our rooms or flats in ways that
make us feel at home, so when our environment is altered
abruptly and without our consent, it is not only unsettling but
our intuition is usually to arrange things back how they were
to recreate our comfy and safe-feeling space.

For thousands of years, societal and religious understanding of family has operated as if it were a historic home,
where if the uninvited were to enter and rearrange all the
furniture—or worse, remove some of it—the curators would
have a heart attack and die at the violation (in manner of
family on *Trading Spaces* returning to find living-room walls
covered in green moss). According to God's law (am speaking generally here), the family *is* what it *is,* and it is *not* to be

meddled with. You can't replace marriage with a loom! You can't replace Mummy's cream-colored walls with thousands of plastic flowers! (Must admit, am gleefully obsessed with anything *Trading Spaces*–related.) Religions are accustomed to operating with a fixed sense of family structure and identity, much like when we return home for holiday visits we assume that our rooms will remain forever as we left them when we first moved away. Family structures have stood rather rigidly across the test of time, and *making* a family is often regarded as the most important right of passage that establishes one's spiritual identity. By rearranging family to fit new lifestyle choices, we face our elders' fears, familial and religious both, that our bending of family in unconventional ways will upset the security it has provided society and tradition for centuries. (V. similar to fear of mums and dads everywhere that they shall return home one day to find that sons or daughters have interior design surprise awaiting them in manner of *While You Were Out*.)

> By rearranging family to fit new lifestyle choices, we face our elders' fears, familial and religious both, that our bending of family in unconventional ways will upset the security it has provided society and tradition for centuries.

Understanding family in a fashion similar to Jewish feminist Laura Levitt's understanding of personal identity might help us better navigate the generation gap we sometimes face on the holidays. While for many years Levitt regarded identity as fixed, learning from her Jewish heritage the centrality and meaning of home with regard to Jewish identity, a series of life experiences (one of them tragic) raised new questions for her about what it means to "be at home" in the self (and, ultimately, what it means to be at home as a Jewish woman). She began to think of personal identity as a kind of "apartment of the self"—one that we can construct, deconstruct, and reconstruct in much the same way that we move into a flat with our belongings, rearrange them at points to create different atmospheres, and sometimes later move out altogether to a place more suitable to our tastes or feelings at the moment. Rather than being like a home that stays the same forever and for all generations to come, our experience of self is more akin to dwelling in a series of homes over the course of our lifetime. (Ideally homes that are bigger, comfier, and with more closet space each time!) Being at home in the self thus requires a willingness to encounter change, not with rigidness but with flexibility, and an openness to shifting to new spaces that accommodate a less-fixed spiritual sense of home.

Women who identify with Ms. Jones along the lines of family must take heart that, though our mummies and daddies may at times react in horror and dismay with regard to our sense of home and family, our generation's role in designing new approaches to family makes us domestic goddesses of a different sort. Inner Poise on the holidays may require us to carefully observe the decades-old expectations from our mums, dads, siblings, and other lovely relatives, in manner of treading lightly on the family heirloom rug. But our generation also faces the exciting possibility of redesigning the spiritual floor plan of family to accommodate new configurations of Singleton life and partnership, rewriting divine law so that it won't collapse if we decide to do things a little differently, making us feel empowered rather than oppressed or left out altogether.

At the same time we must also remember to leave space for those cherished heirlooms we've inherited from our mums and grandmums that we can't bear to lose. After all, despite endless intergenerational struggle, we inherit wisdom from our families that we will probably always cherish, even if this wisdom doesn't quite match our own sense of home as we grow older. (Though sometimes these antiques are better kept in a special place, to be taken out only for special visits of relatives, as said antiques might cramp decorating style . . . but perhaps also might require a shopping trip for that perfect place to keep it!) We face a balancing act of decorating proportions as we try to express our sense of family style in the way that seems right to us, without losing altogether the charm that is our heritage. My own mum did this well in a gift she gave me once. She likes yellow gold and I have always been a silver (or platinum or white gold) girl. For my Ph.D. graduation, she had my grandmother's engagement diamond set on a necklace she had made that was *primarily* white gold (as Mum would never go for silver), but that had little flecks of yellow gold every inch or so. The diamond was all grandma, the white gold all me, and the bits of yellow all her. I was stunned when I saw it—a perfect intermingling of three generations of women, not an easy feat. I must extend a hurrah to Mum for her sense of style and her example on that one!

9

Tick-Tock Goes
the Biological Clock
Is Chick Mummyhood a Divine Fantasy
or Just Religious Fiction?

Number of Bridget's offspring: 0. Number of Bridget's out-of-wedlock pregnancy scares: 1 (v. scandalous). Number of my offspring: 0 (v. good as idea of giving birth petrifying). Number of offspring our mums expect from us in v. near future (perhaps even tomorrow ideally, as mums are getting older every day and not v. quiet about this): as many as possible.

Awaiting the Immaculate Conception

~

A couple of years ago while out to dinner with my parents, the conversation suddenly took a frightening turn, resulting in my intense desire to enact any of the following in utter desperation of escape:

1. Run away screaming, perhaps to the ladies' room
2. Run away screaming, perhaps to the car as walking home not option (too far tottering in outrageous heels)
3. Cower under table and hope Mum thinks have magically disappeared in manner of Harry Potter

The source of this panic was my mother's abrupt mention of her wedding dress. At first, as any daughter would naturally imagine, I assumed that my lovely mum was offering up her vintage gown for my own wedding in preparation of what would be a pivotal event in *her* life (*my* wedding, that is). The fact that I was not engaged at the time seemed irrelevant, as she had decided it was time for me to marry (I wasn't getting any younger you know, tick-tock). Luckily, as far as I knew at the time, my father had not already betrothed me as if I were a piece of property to some random boy with lots of sheep and agricultural potential like fathers did until rather recently in history.

Yet the reality of where my mother was going with the conversation was, in fact, much worse than I had originally expected. What's worse than betrothal to a sheep farmer without my consent, you might be wondering? Well, after quickly dismissing my mother's comment with a reminder that I was not engaged or getting married when last I checked, she reacted in total surprise that I should think her intentions were to offer up her wedding dress for my wearing. *Absolutely not.* Why, of all things, would I assume that (imagine mother's innocent facial expression here)? She was simply letting me know that she was going to have her wedding dress made into a special christening gown for my children to wear at their baptism. Wouldn't that be lovely (batting of mother's eyelashes here)?

The appropriate response to this kind of mummy-bomb-dropping conversation is eloquently expressed by Bridget at various points in her diary, in the form of a loud, "aaaargh" of horror and frustration. My mother had apparently given up on my future Smug Married life and moved right on to the large family I was about to spontaneously produce any minute. After several panicked please-save-me looks at my father, who conveniently decided to stay out of the conversation, I reminded my mother of several things. First, I was not necessarily planning on having children, and second, if at some point I did, I was not necessarily going to need a christening gown, as baptizing fictional offspring was not a given. Then I ran off to the ladies room, muttering under my breath, "Inner Poise, Inner Poise," all the while hoping the conversation would turn to other, less explosive topics while I was gone, like the death penalty or the Middle East—anything other than the idea of my giving birth and the fact that I was approaching thirty.

Mummyhood: A Dream or a Nightmare? "A Wee or a Poo?"

~

Bridget's resistance to the idea of herself as a potential mum provides some of the most hilarious moments in both diaries, including her misreading of a pregnancy test, as well as countless reminders by Smug Married friends and relatives about her ticking biological clock. Bridget *does* share with us some short-lived fantasies about motherhood. During her initial post-shagging-the-boss-Daniel pregnancy scare, she envisions herself as an adorable pregnant woman in manner of Sarah Jessica Parker, coupled with complementary images of Daniel as a loving and sexy father. We also see glimpses of the fantasy when gay friend Tom proposes that Bridget carry his baby, and Bridget entertains brief daydreams about a cute, snuggly newborn available for hugging, Barbie-doll playing, and smelling nice in manner of a baby-powder-infused apartment.

Bridget is well aware that her Calvin Klein–model image of motherhood *is* a fantasy, as is the Catholic Church's Virgin Mary–image of fulfilled womanhood that some of us grow up with. (Thank God, as enduring pregnancy and birth without the sex seems v. unreasonable not to mention highly unlikely.) Unless we happen to be Sarah Jessica Parker or Madonna, who have the buying power of small nations, most of us cannot afford to look *that* cute during pregnancy

> *Sitting under the surface of our psyches was (and still is) the notion that becoming a mother is supposed to express a woman's deepest desire and ultimate purpose.*

and hire an army to help with motherly duties while we maintain impeccable sophistication and fulfilling careers. (As haute couture pregnancy fashion v. nice, but v.v. expensive.) I mean, how many pictures have you seen in the press lately of Hollywood moms in public places with fashionable Paddington blankets draped over themselves for the purpose of at once hiding boobs and feeding a hungry child? That's all the *normal* mothers out there performing this juggling act, as Starlet Mums must have wet nurses to handle this supposedly fulfilling, revered earth-mother-like activity (otherwise known as *milking*). Aside from the glimpse of fantasy, for the most part Bridget is simply horrified by the idea of suddenly having to face children, especially after a nightmarish episode of babysitting her friend Magda's.

Speaking of Magda, her experience of motherhood is almost as painful to watch as Kate Reddy's from *I Don't Know How She Does It* (more on Kate later). In a word of advice, Magda explains to Bridget that she should enjoy her career and the single life, as mummyhood requires exchanging her job for relentless attention to small, needy creatures even on weekends while her husband has affairs with other women and thinks she is on perpetual holiday. Magda's representation as "the mum," as far as Bridget's friends go, leaves nothing to the imagination, as we find her always going on about pregnancy-related infections, wandering in public with her belly in recovery mode (code for: not yet deflated) while dressed in noticeably dowdy "mummy" attire. At one point, Magda is talking to Bridget on the phone while simultaneously fighting with her husband Jeremy *and* realizing her new little one made an unfortunate mess of the bed. "Has he done it in the bed?" She yells at her husband: "A wee or a poo? IS IT A WEE OR A POO?" Ah, the glamorous life of today's mother.

On the flipside, in discussing motherhood I would be remiss not to mention Jennifer Weiner's Cannie Shapiro from *Good in Bed*. Rather than a portrayal of becoming a mum in manner of the depressing Magda, Weiner's is a story of motherhood at once beautiful and heartbreaking. She treats us to the typical laugh-out-loud humor that marks novels of the Chick Lit genre as she chronicles the life of Cannie, a late-twenty-something woman navigating work, men, and her own crazy family. But what makes Cannie Shapiro stand out is that she gets pregnant (by accident) and decides to face single motherhood—a path that is not laughable at all. While I tore through *Good in Bed,* there were moments I couldn't stop the tears from springing to my eyes (tried v. hard to do so as was traveling on airplane). I kept thinking to myself: Cannie Shapiro is so brave! Could I ever be courageous enough to face single motherhood with so much grace? While in the diaries of Ms. Jones, the thought of becoming a mum makes us cringe, with Cannie we are treated to motherhood not as an *ideal* situation but as filled with the complexities of what it means to bear a child and then love her infinitely. Sigh. Mummyhood seems filled with the stuff of spiritual growth: intense grief and intense love, sometimes all at the same time.

Quick, Hide the Fertility Goddess!

~

Traditionally, women have grown up *assuming* that having a baby is part of our future, that at some point we will raise a family, regardless of how long we postpone the possibility. The wildly successful television series *Ally McBeal,* whose protagonist was unmarried, thirty-something, and a successful lawyer, famously and humorously pivoted weekly on her visions of a dancing baby. (Which practically makes Ally a mystic. Having visions, that is. Perhaps dancing baby was really baby Jesus?) These visions were meant to signal that Ally's biological ticking became louder and louder with each passing year, and her fear of never becoming a mother grew. It is not uncommon for a recently engaged woman (not

Smug Married yet, but *engaged*) to be peppered with questions about the date of her impending motherhood, despite
the fact she has yet to even walk down the aisle (people
have no patience with women on this issue!). In college,
though motherhood seemed really far away at the time, I remember how we used to take for granted that we would inevitably have children some day. Sitting under the surface of our psy-
ches was (and still is) the notion that becom-
ing a mother is sup-
posed to express a

*Understanding motherhood
as a possibility, not an
obligation, is a pretty recent
discovery for most women.*

woman's deepest desire and ultimate purpose. A woman's
decision to forego motherhood is akin to fighting a tidal wave
(practically a losing battle and destined to elicit commentary
from all angles that this is v. poor decision and surely regrettable).

Historically within most religions, the experience of
motherhood has been viewed as *the pinnacle* of possible spiritual experiences for women. In the Catholic tradition, devo-
tion to Mary the "immaculate" mum abounds. This idealization
of motherhood has led popes to write various treatises, in particular one called *Mulieris Dignitatem*—a document that glorifies a woman's reproductive capacity in terms of giving her
a special dignity and role in the Church. It argues that in baby-
making a woman encounters her ultimate, God-given purpose. Within Judaism, the role of the mother is prized, as the
survival and perpetuation of Israel rests within her womb (no
pressure there). Further, in the Muslim tradition a woman's pri-

mary function is to produce heirs, and women who bear sons are afforded more rights than those who do not (as men must have sons for their honor within Muslim society). It is not uncommon within these religions to interpret a woman's *inability* to produce a child (often a male child in particular) as a punishment from God or even as evidence that she is *less* of a woman if she does not become a mother.

Moving back a bit in history, even ancient goddess traditions developed around a woman's capacity to give life (but at least it added to a woman's power in society rather than reducing her to empty vessel good only for producing, feeding, and raising offspring). Thousands of years ago, many cultures did not quite make the connection between sexual activity and a woman's reproductive capacity (hurrah for women on that one!). A woman's ability to produce children was considered miraculous and divine in nature, as divinity is usually associated with the power to create. Much of the archaeological evidence we have of ancient goddess culture is represented in figurines procured from digs across Europe of women idols with pregnant bellies, known as "Venus figures," representing the sacredness of women's fertility. Ancient Paleolithic cultures usually traced their ancestry to a deified "Divine Ancestress," revering a female divine-mother figure as the ultimate creator, similar to YHWH. Though ancient goddess traditions also idealized motherhood, feminist retrieval and extensive writing today about the creative, divine power of women once worshipped by *both* women and men has helped women to reinterpret motherhood as a sign of women's empowering fertility, not just in body and family but in all that we do (definitely an improvement).

The Many Faces of Chick Motherhood

~

One of the most significant contributions that Chick Lit (and now what is being called Mommy Lit) makes in chronicling the lives of twenty- and thirty-something women, especially with regard to our spiritual lives, is in its approach to the topic of motherhood. While our mothers' generation came out protesting the housewife mum in manner of *The Feminine Mystique* by Betty Friedan, today women face a somewhat different set of circumstances. For one, many of us have started seeing motherhood *as a choice* and not a given. Understanding motherhood as a possibility, not an obligation, is a pretty recent discovery for most women, and Chick Lit is a major force enlightening us on this point, not to mention helping us to see the complex realities of both joy and struggle on the road to becoming a mum.

Bridget's eye-opening experiences about what it's like to bear and raise children are rather *unlike* the idealized portraits of motherhood handed down to us by Western religion and society. Through Magda, we see Bridget's fear of losing her many-layered, relatively fulfilling Singleton experience. In Magda's portrayal of motherhood, we are reminded of the 1950s mum whose life fulfillment is supposed to rest in her willingness to change diapers and wipe runny noses—not to mention the two years of giving her body entirely over to baby-growing-and-nurturing purposes in manner of the incredibly expanding stomach, followed up by endless breast-feeding responsibilities. Kate Reddy's tell-all chronicling of the high-powered working mum in *I Don't Know How She Does*

It should be required reading for every career girl (and boy for that matter). In her character Kate, Allison Pearson shows us a woman who is forever stressed, never has a second for herself (or her husband), loves her children to death, and feels horribly guilty for not being around, while at the same time would rather die than quit her job to stay home with them. Chick and Mommy Lit are revealing the underside of motherhood (in addition to its complex joys)—a view previously forbidden to women, since for all of history we've been expected to find our Ultimate Fulfillment via the spiritually infused, yet submissive, child-bearing-nurturing experience.

In addition to a more realistic portrait of the twenty-first-century mum, the other major issue that Chick Lit illuminates is the potential conflict between decades of Singleton life and a woman's childbearing years (v. unfortunate biological complication). Whether women want motherhood or not, as we approach and pass that landmark thirtieth year, inevitably our biological clock starts ticking louder and louder. This physical reality leads women like Bridget to go about life in manner of Captain Hook. We begin our thirties running away from a ticking time bomb, trying to ignore that it's following us (the ticking), and shrinking in fear when our clocks are not-so-subtly drawn to our attention by pushy relatives and friends. With every year that passes, the volume of our biological clocks is amplified (I think Bridget's goes to eleven), and with the volume, the guilt intensifies, along with the notion that unless we bear a child soon our whole life is a wash. (Perhaps loudest of all is the ticking in the ears of our parents, as they see the possibility of grandchildren slipping away from their daughter's inability to capture man in manner of Smug Marriage.) For many thirty-something Singletons, life becomes a scramble to get pregnant before our eggs inconveniently run out (or die? Is that what happens? v. bad-sounding), in addition to facing the possibility we won't win the race in the hubby department and perhaps should begin trips to a sperm bank, while letting Cannie's courageous single motherhood inspire us. In addition to all of the above, it seems that we women over the age of thirty are often regarded by men as all wearing blinking signs above our heads that say, "Shag me please! Desperately want a baby ASAP!"

All this talk in the novels of Chick Lit about the positives and negatives of becoming a mum humorously helps us feel out the concept of motherhood in ways previously unimagined. We are still informed by our parents that becoming a parent is the greatest joy we can expect from life, and we live with their assumption that *of course* motherhood is in our futures (even if currently we might hem and haw about the idea). Yet in losing our-

> We can all find freedom in realizing that a woman's creative power expands beyond the having and raising of children, though it may include it.

selves in the characters of Kate Reddy, Magda, Cannie, and even Stacie Trent from Meg Cabot's novels, whose e-mail address reads "IH8Barney" (v. funny as refers to purple dinosaur all kids are obsessed with and all adults seem to find REALLY annoying), twenty- and thirty-something women are indulging the possibility that motherhood *is* a possibility, perhaps the right one for us or perhaps not. And if, God forbid (literally), we pass our childbearing years without actually bearing a child, Chick Lit is also helping women see the positives opened up to us if we do *not* become mothers, including within our spiritual lives (like a life where sleep is retained as a normal part of life, advancing in a career is made easier, not to mention the time to self and significant other in lieu of chasing around little people until utter bodily collapse).

Becoming a Goddess Mother: The Creative Power of Chicks

~

I think all this realism about motherhood calls for a new understanding of fertility to help us along in our journeys toward Inner Poise, which also brings us back to ancient goddess culture and, incidentally, the topic of menstruation (hmmm, interesting). Yes, it's true that ancient goddess cultures sprang from the fact that a woman's capacity to produce life was seen as magical, as idealizing motherhood, and so on. Yet worship of the feminine divine did not *stop* with the motherhood of human life, either. While the feminine divine was worshipped for her *literal* ability to continue the line of a people through having children, the Great Goddess, the Queen of Heaven—the feminine womb—also gave birth to understanding woman as Warrior, Wise Counselor, Prophet, and even the Inventor of Language, as is the case with the Goddess Sarasvati in India. And fittingly for our prolific, diary-writing Bridget Jones, in Celtic culture it is the Goddess Brigid who is considered the patron of language. In Wicca tradition (which draws heavily on goddess culture), the woman's life cycle is represented by the different stages of the moon, all of which have "fertile" or "creative" qualities. During the phase of the New Moon, the young girl is seen as on the brink of reaching her creative capacities, free to take any path before her. During the Full Moon, a woman's creative power sees maturity, and she is fertile, not only in her literal ability to give life in a physical way but in her overall capacity to nurture life, self, and calling. Under the Waxing Moon, a woman is actually considered at the height of her creative capacity, as she is seen as "ripe" with wisdom and power from a life long-lived. (See! At every age we are divinely fertile, spiritually creative people.)

Seeing women in this light helps us understand a woman's fertility as a divine creativity that includes, yet also goes beyond, our capacity to become a mother. It roots women's spiritual identity in an understanding of fertility that exceeds the state of our eggs and can take a variety of forms, making giving birth one among many possibilities. (All v. important for both Singleton women who desire to become mothers yet pass their childbearing years, in addition to Singleton and Smug Marrieds who choose not to have any children at all.) Penelope Washburn, in *Becoming Woman: Menstruation as Spiritual Challenge* (really, this is the title), discusses the symbolic nature of menstruation and of women seeing themselves as creative, fertile beings. Yet rather than call us to wildly celebrate our monthly "gift" in manner of odd ritualistic practices, she expands the symbolism of menstruation beyond literal motherhood to instead symbolize the "fertility" or creative power of a woman's self in all areas of her life. While clearly motherhood is part of a fulfilling life for many women, we can all find freedom in realizing that a woman's creative power expands beyond the having and raising of children, though it may include it as well. Though Cannie Shapiro is a powerful example of a woman who takes an unplanned pregnancy in stride, it is liberating to imagine that a woman may freely choose motherhood in her future rather than be guilted into it by relatives and friends running around after her in manner of crocodiles with ticking time bombs inside.

With all of the above in mind, it is possible to view our heroines Bridget, Kate, Cannie, Becky (and so on) as Fertility Goddesses of a different sort. They stand before us as extraordinarily fertile women—in their careers, in love, and with good friendships, wonderful senses of humor, intelligence, courage, and extensive capacities for self-reflection, as well as a desire to become better, kinder people. Like so many of us, the heroines of Chick Lit show remarkable creative powers that extend to many areas of life, both public and private. Yet also like many of us, they struggle with a life handicapped by the expectation that to fulfill ourselves as women, we must mind our biological clocks lest time run out and leave us barren. Unlike in the past though, we—the audience of Chick Lit—finally have a wide array of portraits of motherhood for the taking, through which we can make informed decisions about how we hope to use our creative capacity. Perhaps it is heroines like Bridget (or shall I say, Brigid, patron Celtic goddess of diary-keeping) who will help inspire us to re-envision our connection to the divine by seeing ourselves as divinely creative both *because* we might literally become a mum but also because our creative capacity may be revealed in so many areas of life, including in places previously unimagined for women (v. exciting!). We become Goddess Mothers, of a sort, by drawing our creative powers into the whole of our spiritual journeys in all that we do and in *all* the relationships we enjoy in our life, be they with children, significant others, friends, or family.

10

All Goddesses Have a Romantic Side (or Ten)

Love, Mr. Darcy, and Loving Mr. Darcy

Number of Bridget's suitors: approx. 4 (including evil-yet-hunkish Daniel, one boy young enough to be offspring, and Mr. Darcy, channeled by Mr. Firth). Number of Carrie Brad-shaw's lovers: approx. 1 million (but Mr. Big wins out, yay). Number of Chick Lit novels not centered on love: 0 (as life is filled with romance. Excellent!).

Mr. Big to the Rescue (Hurrah?)

~

On the eve of not just the season finale but the series finale of the beloved *Sex and the City,* everyone was talking about *the final episode* practically as obsessively as Bridget counts her calories. As I read the Sunday morning paper *that* day (the v. Sunday of the last episode), a photograph of Carrie Brad-shaw, who is played by the famously lovely Sarah Jessica Parker, was the centerpiece on the cover of the Sunday Styles section. In the picture, Ms. Bradshaw is perched in front of her laptop inside her NYC flat, presumably at work on one of her quirky weekly columns. The look on her face is pensive, concerned, and, ultimately, *unreadable*. The photograph evokes a familiar scene for *Sex* aficionados: Carrie engaged in writing her latest newspaper piece, tackling yet another query about love, sex, and the life of the NYC Singleton Girl that determines the theme of each hilarious, often poignant episode about the fashionable martini-loving foursome.

Carrie's unreadable expression in the photograph was intentional, of course. At that very moment, the question on everyone's lips (and when I say everyone, I mean not only all of us who celebrated each new episode in the form of weekly social gatherings but people you wouldn't even imagine would be worried about the outcome) was the following: Would Carrie end up with Aleksandr or Mr. Big, or will she go it alone, after all?

Interpretation: Would Carrie ride off into the sunset with a Man—*any man* for that matter, be it Mr. Big, the above-named artiste, or even David Duchovny's likable yet unfortunately psychosis-laden character, to live happily ever after in traditional Smug Marrieddom? *Or wouldn't she?* Would she forsake the well-trodden path of Smug Marriage for a more permanent Singleton lifestyle? And if she didn't, *what would this mean for women everywhere?* What if a man came to her rescue? What if? What!

With regard to our lovely Ms. Jones, despite the more obvious superficial differences in fashion (I mean, who *really* could compete with Carrie's wardrobe?), Bridget and Carrie struggle with similar questions about the romantic role of men in a woman's life. Bridget yearns for a fulfilling, long-lasting love relationship and snags her Mr. Darcy in the end (perhaps her version of Mr. Big). And like Carrie, Bridget is a Singleton with a career and loving friends who enjoys a good shag now and then, living an independent lifestyle in manner of what was formally reserved only for the male species. By the close of Bridget's second diary and *Sex and the City,* both Bridget's *and* Carrie's boyfriend counts are up to one (since, as we all now know, Big did show up in the end!). While we are left uncertain whether Smug Marriage is in either of their futures, we are fairly sure that love, at least for the time being, *is* (excellent!).

Just Kiss Her! Kiss Her! (Please!)

~

I must confess that I am a shameless lover of love and anything having to do with romance. And when I say love here, I am not simply referring to the substantial kind of love that comes with time and a life with someone (you know the kind that we are supposed to find virtuous, etc., etc.). That kind of love is great and all, but I am also talking about that knockdown, drag-out, romantic, shag-induced love that makes you feel like you are floating along fluffy pink clouds when really you are walking down a gritty sidewalk. Romance induces me into that Zen-flow-like state Bridget describes as "relaxing and going with the vibes," completely allowing me to "live in the moment" as if there is nothing at all except me and the romantic encounter that has me engrossed.

Like many other women, I tear through romance novels in a matter of hours, including the ones meant for "young adults" (as am still teenager at heart). I watch romantic comedies again and again, complete with requisite sigh when the heroine and hero finally get together, *every* time I watch. (Anything with Julia Roberts or Meg Ryan will do, and occasionally a good teenager flick is in order. *10 Things I Hate About You* might be favorite, as it's practically Shakespeare.) A night home alone for me likely includes the following. I take out my favorite episode of *Alias,* from Season Two: The Passage (as am obsessive fan and Jennifer Garner is, in fact, my role model). I forward to the scene where Vaughn (real-life Michael Vartan) *finally* confesses to Sidney (played by role model Jen) that he has secretly been in love with her since the moment he met her:

Vaughn: Sid . . . [said as Sidney starts to walk away from yet another tension-filled conversation, hearing Vaughn saying her name she turns back to face him]. This watch once belonged to my father. It's broken now, but it used to keep perfect time. And when he gave it to me, he said you could set your heart by this watch. It stopped October 1, the day we met.

Sidney and Vaughn look longingly into each other's eyes . . . the moment we have all been waiting for . . .

Me: Yessss! Yessss! Finally! Kiss her! Kiss her damnit!
Sidney's Beeper: Beep! Beep! Beep!
Vaughn's Beeper: Beep! Beep! Beep!
Me: Noooooo! Noooooo! Ignore the Beeper! Gaaaaaahhhhh!

I shout this in manner of a crazed lunatic watching a sporting event who believes wholeheartedly that yelling at the telly will cause the long-awaited kissing outcome. (Yet, unfortunately, no matter how many times I watch and attempt divine intervention, the scene never ends with kissing. But inside I always feel consoled as the long-awaited kiss between Sid and Vaughn occurs in a later episode. Lesson: divine intervention is not fast-acting, and requires patience.)

I *always* want the guy and the girl to get together in the end. The fact that I always *know* they will doesn't stop me from dutifully worrying about the complications that inevitably get in the way. Genuinely worried! I mean, what *if* Meg Ryan never forgave Tom Hanks about the whole putting-her-out-of-business issue in *You've Got Mail*? What *if* Big never declared his utter desire for Carrie? What *if* Jane Austen's Elizabeth and her Darcy never got over all that pride and prejudice? Much like

> *Say goodbye to the wishy-washy submissive girl-bride and say hello to the woman who can think for herself and who finds fulfillment both inside love relationships and outside of them.*

Meg Ryan's character in *You've Got Mail* and Bridget Jones and her girlfriends, I read *Pride and Prejudice* at least once a year, not to mention own the BBC video. Helen Fielding knew what she was doing by modeling Bridget's love life and romantic interest after the beloved Jane Austen classic, as every girl can't help but long for a Mr. Darcy of her own (or perhaps a Ms. Darcy depending on one's sexual orientation).

But what does this romance fixation indulged so wonderfully by the authors of Chick Lit mean for our spiritual lives? Aren't women today supposed to be liberated from *caring* about or *needing* a man (or woman if you are a lesbian) to fulfill us anyway? Aren't we above romance, as romance is really a Hollywood ploy to brainwash women into confusing romance with love and thinking that what will really make us happy is a man? Isn't feeling like we need a man really fifties housewifishness and unbecoming of the liberated twenty-first-century working girl? Am I betraying all of womanhood for admitting that I can't help but rush through all of Meg Cabot's romance-infused novels, because inevitably there is always a Knight in Shining Armor showing up in the lives of her heroines, both teenage and adult? (Noooooo! Nooooo! Am praying to Goddess, please nooooo! Am not betrayer of women!)

Mirror, Mirror on the Wall, What's the Problem with Romance Anyway?

~

One of the major criticisms expressed (often in manner of the v. condescending) about the Chick Lit genre in general, but particularly with regard to Ms. Jones, is that Bridget is just another woman hoping to be rescued by a man. Her desire for Mr. Darcy and insecurities regarding their relationship are viewed as quite unbecoming for women today. Ariana Ghasedi and Andrew Cornell complain in *zmag.org* that characters like Bridget Jones are women who "feel worthless without male validation" and are therefore inappropriate examples for young women; Bridget's need for a man betrays her low self-esteem and inability to handle life on her own. Granted, Mark Darcy often seems to arrive just in the nick of time to "save the day" by getting Bridget that exclusive interview, saving her mum from her latest disaster, or negotiating Bridget's release from a Thai prison (!). But to reduce our femme fatales to "just a bunch of single girls desperate for a man to save them" only succeeds in knocking us off our heady clouds, destroying our Flow (à la scholar Czikzentmihalyi), and returning us to the reality of the gritty sidewalk (not to mention the fact that it completely ignores the independent spirit of their characters). So much for living in the romance of the moment!

Obviously, whether a woman needs or desires a man *is* a relevant question, or we and the rest of the media, not to mention feminists, would stop obsessing about women, our taste for romance, and the pros and cons of Carrie running off with Mr. Big. The fact that it simply *is* a popular topic of conversation does not explain *why* a woman needing a man in manner of Smug Marriage or even just as a temporary significant other is such a loaded question for everyone under the sun, however. Nor does it explain why everyone automatically associates a woman wanting a man as *needing a man for her salvation and rescue.* (Though it must be said that religious traditions have certainly put their faith in men in the salvation/rescue department, as evidenced by the whole Jesus-as-savior thing, not to mention the Father God everyone is always praying to.)

So I have some explaining to do on this contentious topic. To begin, this rather negative attitude about relationships between men and women, as they go off in the lives of our Chick heroines, arises from a concern that these stories somehow affirm the traditional belief that a woman's *primary* purpose in life is to become a good, selfless wife, preferably in the form of a mirror that reflects her husband's every wish. For example, in certain Christian denominations, the man is supposed to act as the *head* of the woman in all matters, both religious and otherwise (this practice would be perfect for a man like Mr. Titspervert, who is not interested in women having heads anyway). While the husband may consult his wife on certain matters, ultimately, all religious, marital, and familial decisions rest in the man's hands, regardless of his wife's thoughts and opinions. All of this womanly submission is, of course, divinely justified, as this Christian view comes straight from Paul in the New Testament, who explains in 1 Corinthians, among other things that

A woman has no head as the man acts as her head (1 Corinthians 11:3)
Woman was created for man and she should cover her head (1 Corinthians 11:7–9)
It is disgraceful (disgraceful!) for a woman to speak in church as it is the man's job to do the talking (1 Corinthians 14:34–35)

(Paul made a lot of problems for Christian women with these types of statements. It's all v. unfortunate.) Thus a woman *today* who allows her interest in a man to dominate her thoughts, which we often see happen in the fictional characters of Bridget, Becky, and others, becomes a red flag for those who are trying to stop what has been religion's prescribed womanly self-understanding from perpetuating itself.

Like Echo, from the myth of Narcissus and Echo, who was duped into a life of "echoing" Narcissus's endless expressions and murmurs of self-love, some feminists argue that through religious and societal ideals, a woman is forever tricked into thinking she needs a man to fulfill her and that, in order to keep him, she needs to reflect just what he wants to see in himself. (Imagine this as other way around: men literally echoing women all the time. Would result in droves of men running around claiming, "Ugh. Am fat in this skirt!" and "Pass me the chocolate, please!") We are raised to dream of Prince Charming, who will one day ride along and sweep us off our feet, supplying our lives with endless joy and love, and fulfilling our every need (simply by his very existence). The romance industry (Chick Lit novels, weddings, movies) is often regarded as a ploy to keep us females convinced that the *Right* man (aka: preceded by the qualifier Mr.) is *the* answer to all our emotional, physical, and spiritual needs. The fear exists that if we aren't able to recognize that the fairytale is really male trickery, women remain doomed to an eternal life of feeding the male ego's need for affirmation and becoming a mirror in which he can find himself and through which he can produce offspring. Chick Lit, for some, is a sign that this is still the situation for women everywhere—that without a man, our lives are incomplete.

Bracing ourselves against love and romance . . . is not exactly the best promoter of spiritual growth and Inner Poise.

Well, give us modern-day girls, not to mention Becky and Bridget, some credit please!

"He Kisses Me with the Kisses of His Mouth" (Yessss! Yessss!)

~

Defending ourselves against romance and love is actually *not* the most productive activity as far as our spiritual lives go. (Hurrah! Always knew romantic-comedy movies and novels were really spiritually infused stories conducive to Inner Poise.) The experience of falling in love, the excitement we feel in the midst of a romantic encounter, and the power of romance to erase the rest of the world from our minds so that no one else exists but our beloved (i.e. the hottie sitting across from us at the dinner table)—these are common ways of describing an encounter with the divine *across* world religions (though the term "hottie" is seldom used in reference to God, I must admit). Romantic love—the kind that is so prominent throughout the genre of Chick Lit, that fluttering we feel in our hearts when we catch that sexy someone looking at us from across the room, is, more often than not, the kind of love used to describe an experience of love that is divine (Yessss! Yessss!).

Particularly within the mystical tradition, be it within Judaism, Christianity, or Sufism, among others, a person's experience of the divine is often described metaphorically as a romantic encounter between two lovers. A mystic regularly expresses an experience of the divine in terms of being flooded with the feeling of love. The mystic's path typically involves a journey deeply inward to the core of the self, with the purpose of uniting with the divine in the most intimate way possible—what some mystics describe as the purest intimacy of all, where the person and the divine literally become one (a v. ecstatic experience). To achieve this ultimate moment requires a certain vulnerability of self. Whether it is a Christian seeking intimacy with Christ, a Jew seeking Kabbalistic knowledge, or a Buddhist monk seeking a nirvana state, a "letting go of self" or "self-surrender" is key along the path to this most intimate of experiences. Without a willingness to open the self for the purposes of experiencing divine love, intense intimacy with God is not possible. The opening of self is not usually instantaneous either and usually occurs along a journey or process, where the mystic learns to become more and more open to the experience of loving God (much like going out on a series of dates, where, as we get to know someone and interest deepens, we are more and more willing to share of ourselves and our past).

And oh, when those mystics finally do encounter the divine, their descriptions of this love experience are quite romantic! One of the most famous romantic (not to mention racy) poems in history is found in the Hebrew scriptures. *The Song of Songs* and its verses have always been particularly popular among mystics to describe their inspired love of God. Christian mystic Bernard of Clairvaux famously ruminated on one of its verses—"He kisses me with the kisses of his mouth"—to describe what was a most heady and weak-in-the-knees encounter with divine love. Hafiz, a famous fourteenth-century Sufi master and poet, described the wonderful experience of loving God as if a game of tag, when in playing, God suddenly "Has kissed you and said/ You're it/I mean, you're really IT!" (Yessss! I'm It! I am really It!) Thirteenth-century Christian mystic Hadewijch, in her poem "Becoming

Love with Love," vividly describes that, "bitter and dark and desolate/Are Love's ways in the beginning of love"—words that oh-so-typically capture the beginning confusion that our Chick heroes and heroines face as they try to navigate their way toward loving each other. In discussing romantic love of the religious persuasion, we cannot forget the famous verses of Jewish poet Kahlil Gibran, who says of love that, "When love beckons to you, follow him" (go! go!) and who urges us to allow ourselves, "To know the pain of too much tenderness," while at the same time remembering to, "Give your hearts, but not into each other's keeping." (As retaining independence also essential to love! See! Romance and independence are not mutually exclusive! Hurrah!)

Up with Love (v.g.!)

~

Bracing ourselves against love and romance and erecting barriers against the heady trip that romantic possibility can induce is not exactly the best promoter of spiritual growth and Inner Poise. Romance is powerful and often just the thing that moves us to open ourselves up to someone else, teaching us about the complexities of what it means to let someone else into our Singleton lives. Loving someone *does* require a degree of vulnerability and willingness to bend and compromise to another's needs. But if we are anything like Emma from Sophie Kinsella's *Can You Keep a Secret,* we will understand romantic love as a two-way street—one that requires *both* parties to participate in a mutual exchange of feeling for that love to work. (Which ideally includes lots of gazing into each other's eyes dreamily, not to mention kissing with kisses of the mouth.) Building walls to shut ourselves off from the way in which romance opens us to another person would end up making our journeys toward Inner Poise rather lonely.

While Carrie, Bridget, and fellow heroines may never be without some romantic interest or other, their fascination with loving a man does not result in the undoing of all that women have accomplished in the last several decades. Telling the stories of Singleton women is affirming the reality that, for the first time in almost the entirety of Western history, there are lots of us who have the opportunity to become who we wish to be while *not* under the watchful eye of a man. For decades even! We are *not* being passed from father to husband in exchange for sheep. While we may not be models of security (I mean, who is, really? We all have our struggles), in our twenties and thirties we are going about cultivating our tastes, our social lives, and our futures with our own money and our own thoughts and opinions in manner of the v. independent. Say goodbye to the wishy-washy submissive girl-bride and say hello to the woman who can think for herself and who finds fulfillment both inside love relationships *and* outside of them.

It *is* true that the good, godly girl may once have been taught (and still is in certain circles and traditions) to freely give up every bit of herself to a higher power, be that father, husband, or god, and that in the past women were raised to be the perfect reflections of the male ego (in depressing manner of Julianne Moore's character in *The Hours*). But the Carries and Bridgets of the world are in a different category of women altogether. While they may love love and be romantics at heart, these are not women who are about to spend the remainder of their lives basking in the shadows of Mr. Big and Mr. Darcy in manner of the Blessed Virgin who is always poised to sit in silent adoration of her famous offspring (i.e. *Jesus,* in case you were wondering). Women today are less and less willing to give up their hard-won sense of self that is now decades in the making. (Ask anyone who has ever moved in with a significant other how difficult it is to suddenly share a space, never mind an entire life with someone, even when love is involved. What happens when you and yours have different tastes? When a favorite chair or lamp is deplorable? When suddenly he puts *brown* sheets on the bed?)

Even Victorian girl Elizabeth Bennett from *Pride and Prejudice* is no mirror to her own Mr. Darcy. Elizabeth exhibits a sharpness of wit, a mind of her own making, and an utter repulsion at the idea of submitting her will to that of a man's, regardless of his noble stature and monetary situation, quite counter to the Victorian age at the time. Ms. Bennett, unlike her supposedly prettier older sister Jane, is not a good candidate for the role of submissive wife. (Which, in the end, and incidentally, is exactly what draws Mr. Darcy to fall madly in love with her.)

Like Miss Bennett, Bridget is about as unlike Mark Darcy as Fielding could make her in terms of humor, opinions, and outrageously endearing honesty regarding life's ups and downs. Which is, of course, why Mark finds her simply irresistible! And which is also, of course, why Daniel ends up wanting Bridget, too. (V. exciting to end up with two sexy men locked in brawl over intense love of same woman as in case of first Bridget movie.) Though at first both Daniel *and* Mark opt to be with what they see as appropriate mirrors of themselves: tall, leggy, tycoon-career women with the right résumé and body, ultimately they both realize that, rather than reflections, they'd prefer someone with a mind and personality (albeit a quirky one) of her own. In lieu of leggy, smug females, they instead both fall for Bridget, quite the opposite of what they initially think will fulfill their every need and desire and certainly not a mirror image of themselves. Hurrah for Bridge! So *yes,* Bridget Jones hopes for a prince of sorts to show up in her life. Yet to reduce Bridget's life, career endeavors, friendships, and adventures, among other things, to be all in the name of becoming a satisfying mirror to Mark Darcy, is to ignore Bridget's character altogether.

> Becoming a Goddess of Inner Poise involves finding that balance of loving and nurturing the self, and loving and nurturing others.

One of the most important things that Bridget's many struggles regarding love and romance teach us is that Inner Poise is not about becoming hard as a rock, able to withstand all temptation, all failure, and all vulnerability in the significant other department. Inner Poise is rather about learning how to nourish the self and, in nourishing the self, discovering along the way the role that others play in both our own growth and our need to contribute to the growth of others around us. Becoming a Goddess of Inner Poise involves finding that balance of loving and nurturing the self, and loving and nurturing others. If we find along our journeys that loving a man (or woman for that matter), in the short term or the long term, is exciting and wonderful, then so be it. Opening ourselves up to love and romance does *not* immediately transform us into a reflection of our lover, as if we are living in a fairy tale. What we see in the heroines of Chick Lit are not women ready to relinquish everything for the man of their dreams but instead women who are learning what it means to hold on to what makes us loveable and unique in the first place, while at the same time yielding to the love and nurturing of another person *without losing ourselves entirely in the process.* (Thus, indulging in the romance of Chick Lit is actually continuing good Inner Poised work, as rereading *Bridget Jones's Diary* is a simultaneous celebration of womanly independence *and* spiritually infused loving! Excellent!)

11

"Human Beings Are Like Streams of Water"

Self-Help, Inner Poise, and Spiritual Epiphany

*Theories about self-help religion: 1 (excellent, am practically spiritual sage). Self-help books thrown in the dustbin: 15 (v.g.? v. bad?). Number retained: 2 (*You Can Heal Your Life, *and* The Road Less Traveled, *v. forgivable). Spiritual epiphanies so far: 0 (but journey still in progress). Positive thoughts about becoming epiphanied: endless (hurrah!).*

"Bridget, self-help books are not a religion."

~

Gloriously shaggable Mark Darcy explains this to Bridget after discovering a hidden cache of books with titles including *Happy to Be Single, You Can Heal Your Life,* and *Buddhism Made Simple*. After sorting through her extensive self-help collection, Mark desires to know *why in the world* Bridget is reading what he believes is seriously lacking in any real value (to put it mildly). In defense of her self-help habit, Bridget claims she has a "theory" about the genre (v.g.), excitedly blurting out that, "If you consider other world religions such as . . ." Bridget has only to utter these few words for Mark to realize she thinks of self-help as a new "world religion." This immediately sparks his dubious if not altogether laughing response to where Bridget's theory is headed. (Clearly Mark is v. unenlightened which accounts for why he is not able to see the truth behind Bridget's progressive and insightful ideas, or as Bridget speculates: "Mark's spiritual soul is not very advanced.")

The conversation between Bridget and Mark leads to what may be my favorite "Bridgetism" about spirituality. As she struggles to illuminate her philosophy of self-help as a new religion, Bridget reflects: "It's almost as if human beings are like streams of water so when an obstacle is put in their way, they bubble up and surge around it to find another path." (Perhaps in much the same way our bodies "bubble up and surge around" tight clothing, in the most unflattering ways, and much to our dismay? Hopefully not.) The obstacle for Bridget here is religion itself, at least of the organized variety, which she speculates is collapsing. She explains to Mark (who we must imagine is looking at her in manner of smug, skeptical male figure yet still incredibly sexy all the same) that human beings seek out sets of rules. If we find that one set doesn't work, we seek out another. Self-help spirituality is helping those people who do not fit neatly into organized religion to find a new set of rules by which to live. Bridget's theory is actually not a bad one, since we *do* seek out structure in our lives, even after rejecting sets of rules that haven't worked for us. Rather than laugh at Bridget, I think we should applaud her character's daring in the spirituality department: she is struggling to understand why alternatives to traditional religion are so appealing to us, even necessary. (It's all v.

tragic that Mark is such an irresistible sex object yet cannot see the obvious possibility in Bridget's hypothesis.)

Christianity is the religion causing Bridget to bubble up and surge around, though the version she inherits seems quite secularized already (despite Mummy apparently having sent her to Sunday school). Her inability to find a comfy place in a religion that abhors premarital shagging and idealizes Smug Marriage in addition to virgin women isn't shocking (virgin mothers, no less, if you are Catholic). The fact that Christianity isn't cut to fit quite as well as a pair of Manolo Blahniks doesn't stop Bridget from participating in Christmas holiday traditions and showing up at church weddings, however. (Even after what we can only imagine are nights of shag-filled happiness with Colin Firth. I mean Mark Darcy.) Neither does the absence of organized religion quell Bridget's desire for a fulfilling spiritual life. In fact, Bridget's own act of bubbling and surging leads her on an intense search for "spiritual epiphany"—a quest not only revered in self-help "religion" but one that grounds spiritual traditions across the world, including within Christianity.

Seeking Spiritual Epiphany Is Like Getting Naked (v. exciting)

~

What Bridget calls spiritual epiphany a Hindu might call unity with the Universal Spirit. Spiritual epiphany for a Buddhist may involve seeking fusion with the Pure Light of the Void and for a Christian entering into eternal marriage with the Godhead of the Trinity. (And for her mum, it might simply require repeatedly saying: "Hakuna Matata" in manner of *The*

Lion King.) Bridget's search for spiritual transformation leads her to focus on hope (i.e. positive thinking), love and forgiveness (v. Christian), enjoying the present moment (v. Buddhist), and reading inspirational poetry (v. cultured?). Bridget casts her net wide in the quest for spiritual enlightenment, not worrying about finding a single tradition and sticking to it and instead piling her journey high with a range of spiritual ideals—sort of a sumptuous religious buffet (that perhaps also includes an open bar).

Spiritual epiphany is often interpreted as a "conversion moment" in a person's journey but not necessarily in terms of converting from one religious tradition to another. In certain circumstances, conversion *does* involve turning to a new tradition, as in *The Confessions,* where St. Augustine "converts" from being a Manichee (not to be confused with the cute sea creatures called manatees) to Christianity. But more often than not, *spiritual epiphany* has a range of possible meanings: from a change of heart that leads to a change in lifestyle or mind-set, to intense purification of the self with the goal of union with the divine, or a Zen-like experience of the Eternal Void. Spiritual epiphany understood as mystical union with God (in theistic traditions) or with the Void (in nontheistic traditions), typically inspires a person toward a more extreme asceticism, which

> The road to becoming traditionally spiritually epiphanied seems to involve getting naked in a multitude of both literal and figurative ways.

may include vows of celibacy, poverty, silence, and an over-all commitment to a monastic way of life. (Obviously, Bridget is not the best candidate for this sort of spiritual epiphany, though she does get excited at one point about The New Celibacy.)

The concept of spiritual epiphany has enjoyed tre-mendous cultural interest of late because so many scholars identify the mystical moment as a place of unity across tradi-tions. Philosophers of mysticism have argued that what mys-tics experience at the pinnacle, or epiphany, moment on the spiritual path, regardless of their religious persuasion, is ulti-mately the same thing. (Hurrah! Grazing at religious buffet is really selfless gesture in establishing world peace! Am saint after all.) Of course, a Christian mystic might describe an epi-phanic experience very differently from the way a Buddhist or a Jew would, due to different practices and beliefs with-in each respective tradition. Yet some regard these distinc-tions as merely the "clothing" of the moment that needs to be "stripped away" to encounter the pure center within the experience. If we strip away the extraneous religious jargon (i.e., the clothing), this leads us to the raw experience that de-fies traditional distinctions between religions. (Excellent! Path to spiritual epiphany is much like provocative striptease be-fore sex! Am convinced.)

In many ways, the stripping away of layers that clothe a spiritual experience is similar to how a Hindu or Buddhist seeks to strip away layers of worldly attachment, desire, and passion, to overcome the pain of human life and reach the Divine Ground or Void. It is well known that even Gandhi put his cause to work for peace above all else, including his family. The reward of spiritual epiphany often leads one to relinquish *all* in a most extraordinary way, giving up home, money, career aspirations, and even relationships, to live a life of poverty in the service of a particular religious calling. (There is even an order of Christian nuns called the Decalced Carmelites, which loosely translates to *nuns without shoes.* Nuns without shoes!) The road to becoming traditionally spiritually epiphanied seems to involve getting naked in a multitude of both literal and figurative ways.

Why Bridget Makes an Odd Buddha
~

Knowing Bridget's preference for Eastern spirituality in her search for spiritual awakening, red flags should be going up everywhere. Let's face it: Bridget is not the best candidate for Buddhahood (at least the Orthodox variety), and, most likely, neither are we (the we here being v. western, twenty- and thirty-something women with careers, significant others, etc.). Rather than visions of naked buddha-ness dancing in our heads, we should instead be crying out: "Forget fashion? Forget desire? Forget passion? What? What!" It's easy to understand why Eastern spirituality is attractive to us materialistic, capitalist Chickies of the *Shopaholic* variety, who compare shopping to "communing with a higher being," despite our suffering finances. But our contact with the East is usually limited to Westernized, self-help versions of Buddhism. Like Bridget, who reads such titles as *If the Buddha Dated* and *Buddhism: The Drama of the Moneyed Monk,* this path sounds much "cheaper," and, according to *Shopaholic* Becky Bloomwood, it will lead us to, "A new, uncluttered, Zen-like life in which [we] spend nothing." (Hurrah?)

Our desire for things—material ones—*does* sometimes overwhelm our consciousness and wallets, as we drop large amounts of money on shirts at Agnès B, in manner of Ms. Jones, or designer chocolates, both hot and cold, at Vosges (if you happen to be me). We have visions of renovated flats and the perfect shag dancing in our heads, de-centering our attention from things like, oh, I don't know, getting to work on time, contributing to charity, and having healthy relationships instead of dating emotional idiots because they make us drool. Conquering our need for worldly pleasure can sound like a quick fix for getting over the loneliness that sometimes accompanies Singleton life, in addition to solving financial crises of *Shopaholic* proportions. (It may also help us accept the mystery of Carrie Bradshaw's capacity to be high-level fashionista in NYC on a writer's salary as simply unsolvable and a fantasy on our part.) Yet I worry that in our attempts to strip away layers of desire, passion, and general human need as the answer to our struggles and in the hopes of becoming, in Bridget's words, "more inner poised and spiritual epiphanied," we may be heading down an impossible road.

Recognizing that we need to tame our desires a bit for a healthier lifestyle is a positive step, especially if we find ourselves, like Becky, praying to the "god of shopping"—a god who can be quite the trickster and lead our lives into utter disarray. But if our spiritual life centers on *conquering* the passions, as in the mystical traditions within Orthodox

Buddhism, Hinduism, and Christianity, then walking this path may feel like walking on a bed of nails while wearing our favorite kitten heels. Armed with Buddhist advice, we can attempt to curb our passions for such things as emotionally unavailable men, alcohol units, calorie-induced obsessions, and expensive shopping excursions as a means of freeing ourselves from the desires that seem to create problems in our lives. Yet if we are anything like Bridget and Becky, who for all intents and purposes remain slaves to their desires, the "set of rules" provided by

> [The] path toward Inner Poise is not a solitary, detached journey of self but one filled with the challenges of constant communion with the world.

Eastern spirituality may not fit us so well in the end (esp. since in ideal Buddhist situation one becomes a monk). A helpful clue to this fact would involve noting that at one point Bridget writes in her diary that she needs to, "get money from somewhere. Maybe Buddha?"

The reality of the Buddhist journey is quite different and more intense than Bridget's self-help Buddhism advises. The "clothing" that is the desire, passion, and general human need that Eastern traditions advise us to relinquish, requires us to give up a lot of the good things in our lives as well. "Stripping away" the distractions of the world to triumph over desire and pain means turning away from not only the cute shoes, Vosges chocolates, and emotionally deficient men of the world, it (ideally) leads to a *general* detachment with respect to the world, both material and human. (Though I have to mention that there are many feminist Buddhists today who are critiquing the validity of this very extreme detachment.) In our attempt to dull the pain of loneliness and soothe the struggles that expand our thighs and weaken our bank statements, I highly doubt our goal is to numb ourselves to joyful nights with girlfriends, long-lasting kisses, and moments of triumph when we find a dress that makes us feel perfect. With the pain goes the joy, with the loneliness goes the humor, and with the peace goes the fun, unfortunately. While it might do us well to find another path, if Buddhahood is not in our future, then where does this leave us?

AAAAAHH! AAAAAHH! Am Sick Soul! (v. bad)

~

Twentieth century philosopher and religion guru William James has a possible diagnosis for our predicament, though it might not sound so good *at first*. According to James, there are three kinds of people when it comes to the spiritual life. First, there are the Healthy-Minded (alas, most of us do not fall in this positive-sounding category). The Healthy-Minded have an almost uncanny capacity to see the bright side of life and interpret situations optimistically. Religion for the Healthy-Minded is not a search or a struggle; it is simply something that one goes along with (in manner of walking down the street singing "la la la") without question.

In the second category, for James, is the Divided Self (oooohhhh. Dark sounding, but still not most of us). The Divided Self is a person who "zig-zags" between commitments and leanings regarding all manner of issues and questions. If fortunate, Divided Selves will eventually come to resolution of such quandaries, as these divisions "ripen" into answers in their consciousness.

Third and finally, is James's category where the likes of Bridget Jones fit the best (though sometimes she can be a Divided Self, too): the Sick Souls. (Uh-oh. Sounds like possibly leads to long-term hospitalization, but with unflattering gowns.) For James, those of us who are born into Sick Soulhood obsess over all kinds of things: jobs, relationships, and decisions both big and small. Sometimes the littlest thing (like not getting a phone call at precisely the right time) can send us into utter despair, but then a happy word can send us into joyous ecstasy. Unlike the Healthy-Minded with their steadfast "la la la-ing," our mantra is better described as "AAAH! AAAH! AAAH-ing" both in manner of seeing our impending doom and utter downfall around the corner at any minute *and* expressing delight at good things. We are filled with doubt in all types of situations, especially about our future happiness, where to find it, why we are here, or the conviction that we are destined to die as lonely, tragic spinsters.

For philosopher Dr. James, however, the Divided Selves and Sick Souls are also the most prone to spiritual epiphany. (Hurrah! An upside!) As a Sick Soul, Bridget is a good candidate for the kind of spiritual enlightenment that leads to a meaningful restructuring of life pursuits, goals, worldview, and religious commitments. In addition to these positives, spiritual epiphany leads to a letting go (for the most part) of what is a rather unhealthy amount of doubt and obsessing, a healing of the "soul's sickness." In many ways, this meaningful restructuring helps a person find that "new set of rules" from Bridget's theory—the set that suits us rather than requiring odd contortions for us to fit (take that, Mark Darcy!).

Hurrah! Am Really Cosmic Sponge!

~

While all of the above have great potential, at least with Bridget we are left with what seems like an unfinished journey toward spiritual epiphany and a perpetual case of Soul Flu. We know that Bridget makes a funny Buddha (as in laughably bad) and that she and her fellow Chick heroines (and we, their fans) probably need a good spiritual remedy. Yet especially with Bridget, her spiritual doubts, obsessions, and struggles are not exactly ever resolved. We have no idea whether she will someday come to rest in a spiritual home, if Buddhist self-help is her final destination, or if she will continue to pile her plate high with a variety of spiritual ideals while steadfastly remaining a woman of the world. We have to wonder, Is she (and are we) doomed to a life of eternal Sickness of the Soul, with an occasional bout of the Divided Self to vary things up? Are our spiritual selves destined to remain clothed in unflattering-hospital-gown attire, or can we find something that better illuminates the spiritual beauty hiding in our worldly existence?

Though much of Bridget's high-level despair and self-doubt may originate from her worldly existence and exposure to the Soul Virus, it is also clear that her joys are experienced *within* the world. It is in her "worldly" interactions and ecstatic exclamations, particularly within her relationships with friends and loved ones (esp. Mark Darcy) and in her finding of success in a career—even a positive interaction with Mum here and there—that we see Bridget at her most Inner Poised. Despite her struggles with Singleton life, her journey is far from lonely or impoverished, and her life is filled with people ready with healing words (and glasses of wine). We meet Bridget as a woman who is *always* willing to give whatever therapy she can to those she cares about, be it in the form of conversation or Cadbury Milk Tray. A journey toward spiritual epiphany that "numbs" her to these desires and feelings might ease the pain of loneliness and despair when they arise, but it would also risk the intense joys of being a Singleton woman of the world surrounded by a community rich with love and laughter.

Imagine if the culmination of Bridget's journey-story *did* result in the achievement of spiritual epiphany, a nirvana-like state of Inner Poise? Would we still find ourselves in Bridget, as so many of us do? Would we find her to be more of a goddess for her newfound ascetic abilities and saint-like restraint? My guess is *no,* and this is where one of the most important spiritual lessons from Ms. Jones comes about. In Bridget Jones we see a woman who is not afraid to look within herself, to diagnose her "sicknesses" (in manner of never-ending lists, among other methods) to see what she needs to change. She is willing to struggle through the difficult life questions that are sometimes scary to ask, especially as a Singleton. Yet in her self-evaluation and struggle-filled journey, we find neither a harsh view of self and the world or a desire to become Mother Teresa. We instead see a real woman who looks and thinks a lot like us, who knows when to ask for forgiveness, and knows when to forgive herself. In her spiritual journey, she never ceases to seek out a fulfilling life *within* the world and *through* relationships with others. Bridget's path toward Inner Poise is not a solitary, detached journey of self but one filled with the challenges of constant communion with the world—a communion she learns she cannot be happy without.

And while Bridget's journey toward Inner Poise and spiritual epiphany may not make her a mystic, there is grace all along her path. In the Christian tradition, grace is often understood as a gift freely given by God on account of God's love of humanity and the world, God's willingness to forgive our imperfections, and our belief that we can turn ourselves toward what is good (despite the whole sickness-sin issue). Taking a nod from St. Augustine (this man was v. complex), Catherine Keller describes humanity and the world in manner of a great "cosmic sponge."

Our challenge is learning to see the grace within and all around us as we struggle along with the ups and downs of Singleton and Smug Married life.

The metaphorical "water" that streams in and out of our porous lives and relationships is, in fact, *grace*. We live in an ocean of grace, expressed through the many ways in which we relate to and love each other and ourselves. Existence is permeated with this liquid substance: we have only to learn to see that this divine grace is flowing all around us and through us. (Hurrah! Was right all along: Human beings *are* like streams of water!)

Thinking of grace in this way, we can begin to see that grace is abundant in Bridget's life. In Bridget, we see a woman who is able to look inside herself and find love despite her struggles, find transgressions but also forgiveness, find imperfection but also hope—a "cosmic sponge" of sorts. And in turn grace flows out of her in the form of love, forgiveness, and hope to all those around her, be they her friends, family, coworkers, or lovers, as they return this gift to her and then some. Though it may not be obvious at first glance, there is grace written all over Bridget's diaries (though v. good that diaries are not literal sponges as would then be v. soggy and even ruinous to our purses).

In our own lives, we have only to look around a bit to see that the stuff of spiritual epiphany is already with us, even if we don't become mystics in the process or resolve our inner tensions about spirituality and meaning in a final way. Our challenge is learning to see the grace within and all around us as we struggle along with the ups and downs of Singleton *and* Smug Married life, discovering the grace that is sometimes hiding between the lines of our own stories. We may not ever reach Buddhahood, and we may even remain vulnerable to sicknesses of the soul, but the divine permeates our worldly existence. Perhaps spiritual epiphany for us Bridgets out there requires the putting on of new glasses—ones that help us to see, in full color and ocean-like beauty, the grace that is written all over our worlds, *even* in those moments when it seems to have departed us forever. (Hurrah! Spiritual epiphany not only allows for worldly happiness but also exciting shopping trip to purchase sexy, spirit-filled glasses in manner of Hollywood movie star. V. befitting of a Goddess of Inner Poise! Excellent.)

Epilogue
Laughing All the Way to My Debutante Ball

Total Celebration Toffee consumed while writing: several pounds (v. bad, but also v.v. good). Total Chick Lit novels read in name of research: countless (am v. proud to get Bridget Jones's Diary *to count as part of day's work). Number of years will most likely continue to write and speak in manner of Ms. Jones: too soon to tell (but suspect v. many as v. difficult to discontinue tendency once begun and is v. habit forming).*

Hurrah! Understanding Book in Manner of Spiritually Subversive Girlie Fiesta!

~

Writing this book has been spiritually liberating: like suddenly getting a huge gulp of fresh air after being stuck under water (though, while wearing v. cute bathing suit). As a professor, sometimes when I slip into scholarly mode with my reading and research, I forget that what women claim about telling stories as a spiritual act has practical relevance (it really works—am feeling spiritually liberated and Inner Poised as direct result of writing this book). When you get a Ph.D., you learn quickly that scholarship is generally supposed to be *serious* business, and the ivory tower image so often used to describe academic life is rather accurate. Going about "being scholarly" can be a very insular experience as a result. (Though, if I ever end up stuck in the tower, I will be the professor with the luscious pink chiffon trailing out the window to alert the oncoming prince of my whereabouts. Or, if not my prince, a large group of girlfriends armed with kitten heels, perfect for scaling those nooks and crannies in the tower wall.)

Along my own spiritual path and in trying to make myself a good religion scholar, somehow I convinced myself that *not* fitting in with the tradition I grew up with (Catholicism) was a problem—something I needed to fix or a phase I had to grow out of. Yet though I love all the saints, the Hail Marys, and rituals of the Catholic tradition, to be truly honest, I have always been more of a "sumptuous buffet" girl in the religion department (am v. much like Bridget in this way). Over the years, I've felt the need to keep my varied spiritual tastes to myself, lest colleagues find out that I am not really a legitimate member of "the club" of traditional religion. (And after copious amounts of research: am certain that membership in any of these clubs does not give special access to anything v. exciting, like for example: secret sample sales.) Writing and researching this book, however, and talking to so many amazing women (Katrina Markoff, Meg Cabot, Amy Richards, and Jennifer Baumgardner, to name a few) about their own spiritual journeys has helped me to realize that where I am on my spiritual path is something to be proud of, not something to hide. I realized that I am in good company with the women of my generation and that our unique approach to spirituality is something to celebrate.

And speaking of celebrating, in the *mujerista* theology (*mujer* means woman in Spanish) of Ada María Isasi-Díaz (a favorite Latina writer of mine if you have not noticed already), she talks about the importance of *fiesta* (i.e. party!) in the spiritual lives of Latina women. She explains that when it comes to religion, Latinas must not only define themselves in terms of struggle (as struggle *is* a prominent aspect of life) and that the fiesta is a liberating, essential part of Latina spirituality. Fiesta, according to Isasi-Díaz, is an occasion when Latinas get together and talk about life, tell each other stories, laugh

> *I am in good company with the women of my generation . . . our unique approach to spirituality is something to celebrate.*

and complain about whatever is concerning them at the moment (in manner similar to *Sex and the City* foursome I would say). This kind of party is a spiritual event (v.g.) where the women involved make the rules and let conversation go where it may.

In light of this fiesta-ritual idea, I have decided (as I recall that authority rests in the self, thanks to Elaine Pagels) that in many ways this book is like a debutante party (note: must purchase dress befitting of occasion)—one held in honor of those of us who, like Bridget, have questions about the spiritual life, who seek Inner Poise but who haven't necessarily found all our spiritual answers in one place. In these chapters I've allowed myself to explore *everything,* no holds barred (spiritual shagging and lusting included), without worrying about whether I've gone too far outside the lines of the traditionally acceptable within spirituality. It feels personally liberating to search for spiritual wisdom in heroines as funny and lovable as Bridget Jones, Cannie Shapiro, Becky Bloomwood, and Carrie Bradshaw—fictional characters whose lives my friends and I actually relate to. The phenomenon of Singleton life is simply changing things quite drastically for many of us as far as spirituality goes, so it seems reasonable to let the likes of Bridget Jones help us along on our way.

And one of my *favorite* things about looking to Bridget as a spiritual guide of sorts has been her power to make me laugh. It is amazing what a good laugh can do for a person's mental, emotional, and spiritual being: laughter can pull us out of frustration, sadness, and anger. It can give us perspective when we've lost it. It can heal our hurt. Laughter is powerful and transformative. The ability to laugh at ourselves and at our friends (not mean laughter but kind, silly, perspective-giving laughter), and at the situations and predicaments we find ourselves in (like imprisonment in Thailand or massively unfortunate tooth accidents) can change our experience in an instant. A good giggle can literally pull us out of despair and suddenly make the world look bright again. Laughter isn't simply a nice vacation (though it can feel like one sometimes); it is also a deep human need, in much the same way that we need food, love, and passions to pursue in life. Laughter is nourishing, both giving it and experiencing it as a gift from others. Even Shakespeare didn't write only tragedies; he wrote comedies as well.

I've had so many experiences of laugh-out-loud moments (in coffee shops mind you) as I've read and re-read
the novels of Chick Lit that my uncontrollable public outburts
have led strangers to stop and ask what I am reading and
why I am laughing so hard. Therefore we must conclude that
laughter inspired by Chick Lit is not only infectious but
community-building, too (v.v.g.). At the moment of finishing
this book, I find myself thanking the goddess that Helen
Fielding had the wit and daring to write Bridget Jones into
existence, not to mention inspire a genre of women's literature in the process. Bridget is quite the interesting and alternative debutante in her own right (especially in the spiritual
sage department), inspiring so many of us to embrace the realities of our lives in manner of a liberating, fiesta-like experience (complete with true confessions, drinks, and lots and
lots of girl-talk). I am thankful to the authors of Chick Lit for
helping readers explore the funnier side of spirituality in relation to our lives today.

The last thing I will confess (as we know confession
is v. spiritually edifying) is my deep hope that you've had fun
at the party and that laughter, with a good dose of spirituality mixed in, has helped you on your own journeys toward
Inner Poise in manner of the v. Bridget. (And that you will
all also hold your own parties and possibly invite me along
as always enjoy a good fiesta and excuse to go shopping for
the perfect shoes to wear at the event!)

A Reader's Guide to the Heroines of Chick Lit

The Syllabus You Won't Find in a Course on Feminist Studies

AUTHOR: HELEN FIELDING

Heroine: Bridget Jones

Bridget Jones's Diary (New York: Penguin Books, 1998)

Bridget Jones: The Edge of Reason (New York: Viking, 2000)

Compulsive journal-writer and object of Mark Darcy's (aka Mr. Darcy) affections, Bridget Jones leaves no detail out as she endeavors to lose weight, curb alcohol-unit consumption, find a better job, and maintain boyfriend count at *one*. Throughout Bridget's adventures we meet her rather nutty mum, her daddy in need of rescue, and lots of Smug Marrieds with kids. But most of all, Bridget tells us of her fellow Singleton entourage and loyal friends: Jude (always crying over vile Richard), Sharon (aka Shazzer, raging feminist), and Tom (gay and looking for love, former one-hit wonder, eighties pop icon). Inspired by the beloved Jane Austen starlet, Miss Elizabeth Bennett, a nineteenth-century woman with a mind of her own, quick wit, and the capacity to turn even the noblest heads of society with her bewitching eyes, Bridget Jones may not be as mannered as her Victorian counterpart, but she is just as lovable and inspiring.

The movie versions of both *Bridget Jones's Diary* and *Bridget Jones: The Edge of Reason* are produced by Miramax Films and star Oscar-winner Renée Zellweger (who channels Bridget perfectly), beautifully brooding Colin Firth (his second sexy Darcy feature film), and hilarious Hugh Grant (as evil-yet-hunkish boss Daniel).

AUTHOR: SOPHIE KINSELLA
Heroine: Becky Bloomwood
Confessions of a Shopaholic (New York: Delta Trade, 2001)

We first meet Becky Bloomwood up to her eyeballs in debt yet seemingly without a shred of willpower when it comes to digging herself out (who can resist a sale after all?). Struggling to gain respect in her job as a financial reporter, find a better career, and avoid all calls and correspondence from credit card and bank collectors, Becky has a lot on her plate. Included on her list of things to do: figure out why handsome PR man Luke Brandon keeps showing up in her life, despite the fact he already *has* a girlfriend!

Sophie Kinsella's *Shopaholic Takes Manhattan* and *Shopaholic Ties the Knot* continue the fashion adventures of Becky Bloomwood (and Luke Brandon, of course). Kinsella's most recent novel is *Can you Keep a Secret,* featuring Emma Corrigan, a Brit like Becky but one who falls for a mysterious American at the office.

AUTHOR: JENNIFER WEINER

Heroine: Cannie Shapiro

Good in Bed (New York: Washington Square Press, 2001)

Cannie Shapiro is apparently what some men call "a larger woman." Or, at least, this is how her ex immortalizes her in a magazine column he titles "Good in Bed" and where he proceeds to describe, much to her utter horror, what it feels like to shag a woman who weighs more than he does. Jennifer Weiner has woven humor, heart, exceptional talent, and a bit of extra poundage into Cannie (i.e. C. as Bruce her ex refers to her on almost a monthly basis)—a character you can't help fall in love with as you live through her ups and downs, mistakes and heartbreaks. Cannie is a woman who breaks off a *long*-term relationship only to regret it later (how many of us have been there?) when her ex has found another woman to love (a little less on the large side, too). Her story ultimately turns on a momentary lapse in judgment that has a rather permanent impact on her life, yet that brings as much beautiful surprise as change and challenges.

Jennifer Weiner's other novels include *In Her Shoes* (New York: Washington Square Press, 2003) and *Little Earthquakes* (New York: Atria Books, 2004).

The television series for *Good in Bed* is being produced by HBO, and the movie version of Jennifer Weiner's second novel, *In Her Shoes* (starring Cameron Diaz no less), is coming soon from Fox.

AUTHOR: ALLISON PEARSON
Heroine: Kate Reddy
I Don't Know How She Does It (New York: Anchor Books, 2002)

Katherine Reddy plays the role of Uber-Woman, juggling motherhood (two kids), marriage (only one husband, thank God), a high-powered financial career (nine currencies, five time zones), and a set of in-laws (too many to name, unfortunately) who think Kate's balancing act makes her a complete failure as a woman. In trying to please everyone but herself, Kate's character offers today's working wife and mother a hilarious-yet-harried vision of the challenges women face when trying to do it all and find happiness somewhere in the middle of all the stress. Be warned: while bitingly sarcastic and endlessly clever, *I Don't Know How She Does It* requires a Kleenex or (six), as her story is heartbreaking in one of those bittersweet ways. (I couldn't put it down and sat stunned for just about forever when I finished it. It should be a must-read for every man on this earth.)

Miramax is planning to release the movie version of *I Don't Know How She Does It* in the near future, rumored to star Nicole Kidman as Kate and directed by Anthony Minghella (who also directed Nicole in *Cold Mountain*).

AUTHOR: MEG CABOT
Heroine: Melissa Fuller
Boy Next Door (New York: Avon Books, 2002)

Melissa Fuller, star of *Boy Next Door,* is a gossip columnist at the *New York Journal* who is always hoping for the opportunity to write a feature but never seeming to get the chance. In addition to worrying about Winona's latest shopping scandals and nit-picking e-mails from HR, Melissa is still a Midwestern girl at heart who believes that getting to know your neighbors is just what one does, even in NYC. Well, being a good neighbor has never looked better since Melissa's willingness to help an elderly neighbor leads to an encounter with what seems like an ideal man. (Though he does have a few identity issues that you'll have to read the book to find out about!)

Heroine: Kate Mackenzie
Boy Meets Girl (New York: Avon Trade, 2004)

In *Boy Meets Girl,* Kate Mackenzie is a trained social worker who ends up in same pesky HR department of the *New York Journal* where we first met Melissa Fuller. An idealist at heart, Kate wonders why she still hasn't opened that free clinic she always thought she would, how she ended up having to fire the *Journal*'s beloved cafeteria baker and pie-maker (against her best judgment), and what to do when she gets caught up in a wrongful termination lawsuit filed by the cookie-maker in question. Of course, sexy lawyer Mitchell Hertzog might ease the pain of being sued . . . though on second thought there is no possible chance that this social worker is going to get involved with anyone as despicable as a lawyer (no matter how nice, funny, and broad-shouldered he is).

Heroine: Samantha Madison
All-American Girl (New York: HarperTrophy, 2002)

While perusing CDs at a local music store one day, Washington, D.C., girl Samantha finds herself in a shocking situation.

Before her very eyes, a suspicious man across the store is readying himself to assassinate the president, who has just pulled up in full entourage outside! So she does what any girl would do—she saves the leader of the free world . . . and suddenly finds herself a national celebrity, invited to every party at school (by all the girls who wouldn't give her the time of day prior to her presidential rescue), made a teen ambassador to the U.N. (what?), *and* given to thinking continuously about the president's son David (who would have thought he wasn't a geek?). Samantha is teenager girlhood at its best: sarcastic, wanting to save the world (and even having a chance to do it), and as obsessed with boys as any other girl her age (or girl who happens to be twenty- or thirty-something, ahem).

Heroine: Mia Thermopolis
The Princess Diaries, Vol. 1 (New York: HarperTrophy, 2000)

What would it be like to go to bed one night an ordinary teenage girl and wake up the next to find out you're the princess of a country (albeit a small one, but still)? Such is the fate of Mia Thermopolis, an activist, outspoken girl, muddling her way through high school, worried about boys and her mom's latest dating adventures, who's just about the last person on earth who would want a royal title to add further complication to her already challenging existence. Mia journals away with sarcasm and witty observations about the trials and tribulations of becoming a princess, for real.

The adventures of Princess Mia continue in *The Princess Diaries,* Vol. 2: *Princess in the Spotlight;* Vol. 3: *Princess in Love;* Vol. 4: *Princess in Waiting;* Vol. 4½: *Project Princess;* Vol. 5: *Princess in Pink*

Also the movie versions of *The Princess Diaries* (both 1 and 2) star Anne Hathaway as Mia and Julie Andrews as her Queen, princess lesson–giving grandmummy.

AUTHOR: LAUREN WEISBERGER
Heroine: Andrea Sachs
The Devil Wears Prada (New York: Broadway Books, 2004)

Andrea Sachs has got it bad when it comes to work! Her first foray into the world of work lands her what everyone tells her is the chicest, coolest job that every girl would just die to have: personal assistant to the famous (or rather infamous) Miranda Priestly, editor-in-chief of *Runway Magazine*. Poor Andrea thinks that doing her time at *Runway* (which includes the most outrageous and degrading tasks you've ever heard a boss ask an employee to do) will land her a coveted writing position somewhere like the *New Yorker,* but as it turns out, the job that every girl would die to have may just end up killing her for real (not to mention completely jeopardize her love life).

AUTHOR: KRISTIN GORE
Heroine: Samantha Joyce
Sammy's Hill (New York: Miramax Books, 2004)

Samantha Joyce, unlike our typical heroine who seeks the spotlight in the publishing or television industry, lives the life of a harried Senate aide up on Capitol Hill in Washington,

D.C. While at first glance the trials and tribulations of a health-care analyst for a senator from Ohio may not seem terribly glamorous, any girl who's ever been into politics inside the beltway (I actually lived in D.C. for twelve years) knows that working on Capitol Hill can make for a very interesting life-style (especially among all the many cute staffers one runs into from both the House and the Senate). So in addition to health care, we find our heroine Sammy thinking an awful lot about a certain speech writer, Aaron Driver, who happens to work for the senator running against her boss (oops). With *Sammy's Hill,* readers find not only romance but an alternative perspective on women in the workplace, specifically the world of U.S. politics.

AUTHOR: ELIZABETH YOUNG
Heroine: Harriet Grey
A Promising Man (and About Time Too) (New York: Avon Books, 2001)

Once victimized by gossipy, manipulative, perfect childhood "friend" Nina, Harriet Grey of *A Promising Man* suddenly finds herself out for drinks with what seems to be Nina's boyfriend (who is also rather cute). Harriet is a woman surrounded by her friends—literally, since she lives with the best of them in manner of college roomies in a rather large townhouse that she owns. As her mood and life are complicated by the ups and downs of those in close proximity, particularly single-mum-friend Sally (whose son also lives in Harriet's house), Harriet comes up with lots of excuses to keep John Macken-zie (Nina's apparent man) at arm's length. After all, who needs to be fixing sights on a man already taken by a woman who would kill if she knew someone was after her boyfriend? Such are the romantic quandaries and adventures of Ms. Harriet Grey.

Elizabeth Young is also the author of *Asking for Trouble* (New York: Avon Books, 2001).

AUTHOR: LESLIE STELLA
Heroine: Lisa Galisa
The Easy Hour (New York: Three Rivers Press, 2003)

Lisa Galisa has big, glamorous dreams for her life (not to mention that she is rather on the big side as a person, too), yet she fears she will forever remain a saleslady at the local Chicago department store she has been working at for years, stuck reliving the lives of her parents. Then Lisa gets a star turn at portraying glamorous Maria Callas in a special couture promotion in women's wear, which gets her noticed by Chicago socialites and her menswear Aristotle counterpart alike (who turns out to be quite the sexy catch). Lisa is a woman who struggles to hide her blue-collar roots, yet in the end faces choosing between what feels right, despite all her efforts to the contrary (both workwise and guywise) and the socialite life she always dreamed of having.

Leslie Stella is also author of *Fat Bald Jeff* (New York: Grove Press, 2001).

Kindred Spirits

Conversations with Some V. Cool Real-Life Chicks: Katrina Markoff, Meg Cabot, Amy Richards, and Jennifer Baumgardner

A CONVERSATION WITH KATRINA MARKOFF
Chocolatier, Owner, Vosges Haute Chocolate

Katrina Markoff, owner and executive chef of Vosges Haute Chocolate, creator of Celebration Toffee (C.T.) herself, has been dabbling in delicious delicacies all over the world. After graduating from Vanderbilt University in Nashville, she attended culinary school at the prestigious Cordon Bleu. The extraordinary success of Vosges is due to her adventurous and creative approach to the possibilities of chocolate: for the body, the palette, and spirituality. Please visit www. vosgeschocolates.com for more information about Katrina or to order some of her yummy creations, or stop by in person at one of her many stores across the United States.

d.f. How did you get into making chocolate?

k.m. I went to cooking school at Le Cordon Bleu in Paris. They do not have an extensive chocolate-making program since in the haute cuisine world there are mostly pastry chefs. So I am self-taught. What I find exciting is that when you teach yourself you become more creative, come up with your own methods. In cooking school, they didn't want you to go outside of the box, but when you don't have the training in something, you *have* to start outside the box.

Actually, I didn't have a thing for chocolate until I went to this restaurant, L'Ambroise, when I was living in Paris with two friends. After dinner, they served us little round Beignets that were crunchy on the outside with a burst of chocolate when you bit into them. It was truly an *Oh-My-God!* chocolate experience. I hadn't known until then that chocolate could be so sensual and shocking; it was almost a sexual experience. There was such an element of surprise—it was amazing. I liked the contradiction of the salty crunch next to sweet liquid chocolate. This experience had a huge impact on my understanding of chocolate and is the reason I pair things like balsamic and chocolate. And it's because of this eating experience that Vosges became Vosges—the restaurant was located in the Place de Vosges in Paris.

I also went to live in Spain and worked with this chef who encouraged me to use my imagination and palette as my guide. Then I began traveling around the world. I went to Thailand and India and was inspired by all of the spice markets and exotic fruits—I wanted to incorporate these spices in my chocolates—to draw all these amazing places into the experience of chocolate.

d.f. So, what's the best way to eat a chocolate, according to Katrina Markoff?

k.m. My favorite *time* to eat a chocolate is in the morning, because your palette is so unadulterated, clean, and pure, with the rising morning sun. When you wake up in the morning, you tend to be a little bit slower. Hopefully, you don't have a lot of things on your mind, because you've had a nice rest. So if you can, take a moment and eat that chocolate of choice—so slowly. Of course, for me, how you would eat it depends on the *kind* of chocolate. If it's a truffle, I always make sure to eat it in at least two bites, because I love looking into what I just bit into, seeing the texture of how your teeth made marks in the ganache. And once I put chocolate in my mouth, it's really important to breathe, because you taste things through your sense of smell, and just like when you bring air into wine, the flavors become much fuller and much more apparent in the chocolate. I like to have my eyes closed for the first bite, because again, it's reinforcing the whole "what's going on inside your mouth" idea.

d.f. With regard to chocolate in particular, a big issue for women like Bridget Jones (and maybe me) is that they love, love, love chocolate and food but then obsess about calories and weight. What kind of advice do you have about chocolate in relation to our bodies?

k.m. I like to think that when I put food in my mouth I am putting energy into my body. So I would rather eat a sumptuous chocolate than a piece of fried chicken thigh. Chocolate has such a mystical history from the culture of the Aztecs. And then with the things I do with chocolate—like using curry from India and kaffir limes from Thailand—I hope that there is an even more exotic transvergence of energy into the body. When I have my chocolate or any food, I try to make it a spiritual experience—as long as you're putting good ingredients into your body then eating is a good thing for you to do.

d.f. One of the things I love about Vosges is that you approach chocolate as a way of life, almost ritualistically. So how then can eating chocolate be a spiritual, ritual experience?

k.m. If you can give people a reason to slow down and have a ritual, intimate experience with their body through food, you can make eating into something sensual. And with something as decadent and naughty as chocolate, it becomes a spiritual experience.

It's also all about the breathing, I think. When you take deep breaths it slows your whole body down. It is amazing what our bodies can experience if you give them a second. So often the mind and our schedule take over, but if you slow down and take a bite of chocolate, pay attention to its smell and how it feels in your hand. Chocolate is unique because instead of using a fork, which is just this metal object between you and your food, with chocolate you use your hands and you feel it melting against your fingers. How often do we use our hands to eat? Almost never—so paying attention to this fact is amazing. As chocolate melts, it inspires you to lick your fingers, which can take you back to your childhood, when you were licking the bowl as your mother was making brownies.

It's this ritual part of eating chocolate that led me to associate chocolate and yoga. The ritual of eating a choco-

late can *be* the yoga—the thing that gets you into a medita-
tive state. Doing yoga by yourself is a one-on-one experience. And, like yoga, chocolate is one of those things that
when you eat it by yourself, there is something really intimate
about the process (if you let it be): it becomes a medium of
spiritual experience.

d.f. Speaking of yoga, what vision led to your development
of a chocolate/yoga retreat? (chocolate and yoga?!)

k.m. A friend of mine from college inspired me to do this.
Vosges had just moved from a warehouse into this new
window-filled space. I decided that one room had to be reserved for yoga because I wanted my staff to have access
to yoga in the workplace. So we started doing yoga every
Wednesday at 5:30, and anybody could come, even friends
of staff. Our teacher has this amazing voice, and she would
play music and we'd all be hugging at the end. After class
one day I decided that I was going to have a chocolate, and
I was blown away by the experience of eating chocolate
after just having done yoga. I was so into my body in that
moment—my hips, my thighs, my insides—so when I suddenly had a bite of chocolate, it was a whole new experience. It was amazing the flavors that came out after that
class. So it sort of led me down that connecting path of yoga,
of spirituality, of ritual, and of chocolate. I just thought there
was a real connection.

   So then I called my friend from college who now runs
a yoga studio to talk about the idea of doing yoga-and-
chocolate retreats. I was thinking that maybe in certain poses

you'd hold on to certain textures, like flowers, or you'd experience certain smells, and then at times you'd listen to
music. The overall idea is that we are unifying spiritual prin-
ciples through food. My friend loved the idea, and now we
have this retreat in Oaxaca—a place in Mexico that is associated with chocolate. For the retreat, I knew I not only wanted
to get foodies who hadn't done yoga before to try something
new and experience chocolate while doing it, but I also wanted to get yogis, who tend to be pretty strict in their dietary regimens, to be open to having a little fun and trying something
a little bit different and not always be so serious, since some
yogis are *really* serious.

d.f. Characters like Bridget Jones are always looking to Eastern spirituality and Zen for all of their spiritual advice, but
then, at the same time, they just make the worst Buddhas, because they are all so indulgent and full of desire! Yet we look
to Eastern spirituality to enhance and open ourselves up beyond our comfort zones, while at the same time challenging
the person who practices Eastern spirituality to open themselves up to the lighter side of things and indulge a bit.

k.m. I know—it is so interesting, because very rarely do
people challenge the yogic-Buddhist-Hindu side of things. If
you want *real* spirituality, there is a sense that you have to
follow a strict form of being a yogi or a Buddhist, yet it's so
interesting to lighten it up a bit. I think we can still keep the
spirituality but in a way that is not as serious and stern, which
I think is appealing to a lot of different types of people.

d.f. How do you see the role of spirituality in terms of your own personal growth and in your experience of the work that you do?

k.m. Well, my mission with Vosges, in so many ways, is to really shake things up for people so that they think outside the box right along with me. So I make these wild flavors from these exotic cultures, drawing them into this medium of chocolate. And I think, spiritually speaking, my mission is to bring people together, and at the same time open their minds to new experiences, to things that they've never seen before, things that they've never conjured up in their heads as something that would go together, that would work together. When you give someone curry and chocolate, sometimes at first they say: "Oh my God, that sounds disgusting." But then if I can get them to try it, all of a sudden they're open to all these other combinations that before seemed so wild. So I hope that my chocolates inspire people to become more open to trying new things, and I think that this kind of willingness is what leads to a more unified and interesting world. Then we don't stay living in these boxes.

A CONVERSATION WITH MEG CABOT
Author, *The Princess Diaries, Boy Next Door*

Meg Cabot is a wildly successful writer among both the teenage and twenty- to thirty-something female audiences (quite a range, I have to say). A graduate in fine arts from Indiana University, Meg is famous for her series *The Princess Diaries,* which has two (!) movies to its credit, as well as her novels of the Chick Lit variety, *Boy Next Door, Boy Meets Girl,* and *Every Body Has One*. All of her stories feature highly empowered women with great taste in men *and* who are making a difference in the world (v.g.). See her movies, read her books, and learn more about her at www.megcabot.com.

d.f. What inspired you to write and keep writing?

m.c. Since I *could* write, I've been writing stories. It just never really occurred to me that I would get published. I had thought about it, but I grew up in a college town and I knew a lot of professors so I also knew how difficult it was to become a published writer. I never seriously thought about it until my dad died suddenly in 1993. When that happened, I thought to myself, "Wow, you don't have a lot of time in life, so if you have something you want to do you better start doing it or otherwise you may never get the chance." So I started buckling down and writing a novel and looking for agents right after I got home from the funeral. By about a year later I had an agent, and in 1996 I got my first book deal. After that I just kept writing because I can't stop. It's really fun that I get paid for doing what I enjoy doing anyway, so it's a fabulous career.

d.f. What do you think are some of the most significant struggles your characters face as they go through their lives?

m.c. I think they face the same struggles everyone faces. They're trying to find their place in this world, and they're constantly being bombarded by all these negative challenges. So they've all got to learn to somehow deal with the negative in a positive way. I am thinking here especially of the teenager heroines and some of heroines I'm writing for adults: they are constantly being thwarted by evil people, trying to find their way in a positive manner while getting all this negative feedback from the world.

d.f. Who are some of the evil people that they encounter?

m.c. Human Resources employees [laughs]. It just seems like there are a lot of people out there for themselves only and not so much looking towards what's good for everyone else. From middle school onward I've constantly seen girls who are totally into themselves and self-absorbed, who don't care what they say and what impact they have on others. You know: mean girls. And mean girls grow into mean women. Some of those girls who are mean in school and lord things over others suddenly become the woman who is your boss, who likes to pick on you. The characters I write about are just trying to do the best they can, even while others keep trying to find ways to put them down.

d.f. So they're struggling in the face of some very negative energy while trying to retain their positions and keep a sense of humor about everything?

m.c. Exactly! Some girls just don't get it! They forget about the love in the world; they forget about Karma. I absolutely believe in Karma—that the vibes you send out in this universe come back to you. I think people should always try to do the right thing, and if they don't, it will come back around to haunt them.

d.f. When you invent a new character and story, what do you hope your readers take away from your heroines and their adventures?

m.c. I hope readers get a sense of empowerment, that even if you are just a teenager walking down the street (like Samantha Madison in *All-American Girl*) who sees someone trying to kill the president, that *you can't just stand there*. You have to do something! There are parallels like this in all the stories I've written. My characters always end up making a difference in people's lives because of who they are and the fact that they don't crumble, even under peer pressure. I hope girls get the feeling that they're not alone and that everyone faces similar challenges at one point or another, especially when we are teenagers. I want my readers to feel like everything will turn out OK.

d.f. What about for some of us older women?

m.c. Well, it's basically the same. You can have the worst boss in the world, and you *will* persevere in some way. Someday that person will get what is coming to them.

d.f. The heroines in your novels share similar struggles with Bridget Jones about body image, family, men, and so on, but they also have a much wider sense of the world; they all seem to want to save the world somehow. Mel cares for her elderly neighbors, Samantha stands up to the president in the art contest, and Mia spends spring break doing "housing for the hopeful." Why do you always write this quality into your characters?

m.c. As a writer, I often feel like I'm an observer in life, so I like to write about characters that are different than me, who actually go out and try to make the world a better place. I try to send this message out to girls and women—that you can make a difference in someone's life. We can't only think about ourselves, and we need to be able to empathize with others who aren't as lucky as we are. I think it's important to remember that we're all here by the grace of god, so we should always try to help others. Someday that person in need could be us.

d.f. Are you hoping to inspire your audience to think about larger issues that are going on in the world, in addition to finding boyfriends (which is, of course, also very important)?

m.c. I do try to do this but in a really entertaining way. My goal is that people won't exactly notice the message I'm sending but that somehow the message will end up influencing them before they even realize it. Then I know I've done my job. I want to get a message across, but in a believable way. Bridget Jones in particular struck me as the kind of person who is always trying to do the right thing and be kind to others. I think Helen Fielding did a great job in making that dimension part of her character.

d.f. One of the things I talk about in *Becoming a Goddess of Inner Poise* is how Bridget's diary-writing is a spiritual act. Especially within women's spirituality, a woman voicing her story is considered spiritually powerful and transformative. Writing in journals, making lists, and writing e-mails are central to all your characters' identities. Why do all your characters write so much?

m.c. Well, girls like reading stories in the first person; they feel so current. It's as if we get to read the story as it happens, as opposed to getting a book that's written in the past tense with an omniscient narrator. I think there is also a voyeuristic quality to it; we can connect to the story that much faster when it's a diary.

d.f. If you were to think of your characters as spiritual role models, what might they teach us about the spiritual life, if anything?

m.c. Well, all my characters are influenced by Karma. I think they worry about cosmic retribution and the importance of treating others as you want to be treated. People write to me all the time asking me what religion my characters are, and I really try not to answer this in a specific way because I want my characters to be universal. I really have to say that I'm not pro any one religion. Though the one thing that I see all religions have in common is that you should try to treat others the way you want to be treated, and I hope my characters express this ideal.

d.f. Do you have any spiritual guidance you would like to leave the readers with?

m.c. I do think that especially considering what's happened in the last few years, with my dad dying and also being in New York and having been here in the year 2001, I think that you really need to seize the day. If there's something that you've been wanting to do, you should do it. Don't wait around for the perfect time because that time is never going to come. For so long I was paralyzed with the idea that if I got a rejection letter, I would just die, and it's simply not true. You just don't know until you try something. Do get out there and just do it—it's kind of like the Nike ad.

A CONVERSATION WITH AMY RICHARDS
Coauthor, *Manifesta: Young Women, Feminism, and the Future; Grassroots: A Field Guide to Changing the World*
Founder, The Third Wave Foundation
http://www.soapboxinc.com/bio_amy.html

Amy Richards has made quite a splash as a spokesperson for a younger generation of feminists. A graduate of Barnard College, Columbia University, and an occasional consultant to Gloria Steinem, Amy is involved in a long list of ongoing projects, including an online column called "Ask Amy" at www.feminist.com and The Third Wave Foundation, which she cofounded, as well as writing *Manifesta: Young Women, Feminism, and the Future* and *Grassroots: A Field Guide to Changing the World* with her friend and colleague Jennifer

Baumgardner. Read more about Amy at http://www. soapboxinc.com/bio_amy.html.

d.f. Can you begin by talking about why you and Jennifer wrote *Manifesta*?

a.r. After cofounding The Third Wave Foundation and through my online advice column "Ask Amy," I realized that people were interested in feminism but confused about what it meant. People were constantly asking: What is feminism? So Jennifer and I decided that there was this need to document the feminism going on among our peers and for our generation.

d.f. One of my favorite things about *Manifesta* is that the first thing your readers see is your dedication: "To feminists every-where, including those of our generation that say 'I'm not a feminist, but . . .' and to others who say 'I am a feminist, but . . .'" which are both statements I hear from my friends, college women, and myself all the time. What do you say to a young woman when she tells you she's not a feminist?

a.r. I usually try to figure out what in her life might *already* be feminist, . . . to show [her] that feminism is already a part of [her] life. As my friends now advance in their careers and relationships, those who didn't think they needed feminism are finding more and more that they do. This happens espe-cially among women who are most conventionally success-ful: they work at investment banking firms and got out of the gate really well, but now they're criticized for leaving at

6 o'clock, *and* they're criticized for not being good parents. I find that as women get older they realize how important feminism is to their lives and how much they need a sounding board for feminist issues.

d.f. How do women today reconcile their feminism with the fact that they've got careers and they read *Vogue* and they scream over shoes in shop windows? Do you think that the word feminist needs to be rethought or that we need alternative words to talk about it?

a.r. I definitely don't think that we need a new word because I think that, regardless of what we call it, there's going to be confusion about what we mean when we say "feminism." Feminism isn't just one thing, yet we always think, "Oh, a feminist is someone who *only* reads *Ms.* magazine." I think it's fine to read *Vogue and* be a feminist. I can't underscore enough how often I get asked those questions: "Can I be a feminist and read *Vogue,* can I be a feminist and get my bikini line waxed, can I be a feminist and like boys?" That gets exactly to the "I *am* a feminist, but . . . I have all of these things that make me seem a little bit of a hypocrite."

We don't live in a perfect society, and there's no perfect definition of what a feminist is. Last night a friend got engaged, and she has her huge diamond ring but says that every time she looks at it she thinks of starving children in Africa. In response, I told her, "But you do so much good work! You do *not* have to worry about it. We're allowed indulgences. And even if you didn't have that ring, you're not going to solve the problem of starving children in Africa."

Even *if* you stop reading *Vogue* there are still going to be women who are anorexic.

We need to remember that we also grew up with a critique of what it means to read beauty magazines and feel seduced by them. Because we have the consciousness, we know we're being sold these things. I don't think it's as damaging for our generation to read it. We also need to each realize what our individual power is and that we can read *Vogue* and wear the diamond ring but also give money away, talk about body images, decide not to buy sweatshop-labor-made-clothes—do whatever we can and realize you can't be perfect.

d.f. I'm going to shift and talk more about Bridget Jones as a character and the Chick Lit genre in general. Helen Fielding's character has enjoyed such popularity among women, and that spawned this whole genre of writing by young women. What do you think of Bridget and the women of Chick Lit?

a.r. Well, first, I suppose you could argue that Bridget Jones really laid the groundwork for *Sex and the City*. And I did read *Bridget Jones* when it came out and loved it, and so many of my friends did as well. They would write their e-mails as if they were Bridget Jones, and it really just caught on. I actually think that the Singleton life is a real fantasy thing; it's someplace that we all want to go to in a sense of wanting to be free and independent. But it's a place that very few people actually want to be for the rest of their lives. I think Helen Fielding really captured that—the freedom yet all of the insecurities that go along with it.

I was actually over in England right after it came out, and I met with a woman named Natasha Walters, who wrote this book called *The New Feminism*. I asked her about how Bridget Jones related to her work. She said it was really fascinating because she worked at the *Independent* where Bridget Jones was first released, and Helen Fielding was the first woman columnist ever at this paper. She said that her largest point of contention about the column was that no one talked about what a brilliant piece of writing this was. Everyone was just seduced by this character; everybody talked about what a sell-out it was to feminism.

d.f. One of the struggles that younger generations of women face with regard to religion is that many of us don't fit the profile of the good religious girl anymore. So we end up like Bridget Jones: spiritual-but-not-religious. What do you think of this real interest in spirituality by women that falls outside traditional religion—more of an Oprah kind of spirituality?

a.r. I think what most people are looking for in religion or spirituality is a community and a belief system. I think everyone wants some form of that, just confirmation that what they're doing isn't bad or evil or wrong. I think it's hilarious when I'm in a conversation with someone who says, "I can't do that, I'm Catholic." Or "I would love to support abortion but I can't because I'm Catholic." And yet these are the people who I know are having premarital sex. I think religions have already become something that we pick and choose to match our personal belief system, but yet we're dependent on them in the larger world. Historically, the feminist approach to organized religion was to oppose it because there was this assumption that if feminism was about dismantling patriarchy, organized religion was the epitome of patriarchy. So feminists felt that they couldn't be both feminists and religious. I think what's changed is that many feminists left their religions and actually felt incomplete in some way. So then they said, "This didn't really solve my problems. I feel in fact worse, because I feel like I've left a part of myself." And then what feminists tried to do, and did successfully, was get at the roots of all these religions and discover what about them was good. Now there are groups like Catholics for Free Choice and writers like Hyung Kyung Chung and other people who are saying it's not the religions that are bad, it's the interpretations that are bad. I think that this is where our generation of feminists has entered the conversation. We know that we don't have to reject religion in the way that previous generations had to reject their mini-skirts.

d.f. The "spiritual-but-not-religious phenomenon" in our generation has sent a shockwave through older generations, who worry about how we feel we can pick and choose what about religion fits us and what doesn't, what we can accept and what we can reject. There's a sense among older generations that either you take it whole or not at all and also a sense of loss that people are taking all this liberty with religion. What do you think of this?

a.r. I don't ever want to reject the entire thing [religion], so then the question becomes, how do you do both? I think it's not unlike what makes Tony Blair so popular—the "third way" of politics. Religion is like politics. Young people are grappling with not wanting to be a Democrat *or* a Republican. It's the same thing as not wanting to be a Christian *or* an atheist; they want to be somewhere in between.

d.f. Last question: Do you have any spiritual wisdom to leave our readers with?

a.r. I think the reason that people feel so conflicted about the feminine things in their lives is because they haven't yet figured out how to own their feminism. I once spent a lot of time debating about "oh my gosh can I have that 90210 party if I'm a feminist?" but then the minute I just started doing so much feminist work, I realized that these kind of worries were pointless. My work speaks volumes beyond the fact that I wear perfume every day. (And yet talking about perfume de-legitimizes me, so [I] just do those things and don't talk about them.)

On the spirituality aspect, I think people should figure out how to work within the system rather than always fighting the system. I know with feminism I used to walk into the room, and I would assume everyone wasn't a feminist and I would think, "OK, who am I going to have to fight with, and who am I going to have to convert?" and now I walk into a room and I presume everyone is a feminist, even though if I really thought about it I know that most people aren't comfortable with that label. But I just use that as my approach, and it makes me have much better conversations. So, presume the world isn't working against you. Presume, as a Catholic, that the Vatican isn't anti-woman and see what you accomplish from those places. But then only leave them or reject them once you have exhausted all the possibilities. I think you have more power from the inside out than being an outsider complaining.

A CONVERSATION WITH JENNIFER BAUMGARDNER
Coauthor, *Manifesta: Young Women, Feminism, and the Future; Grassroots: A Field Guide to Feminist Activism*
http://www.soapboxinc.com/bio_jennifer.html

Jennifer Baumgardner began her feminist activism at Lawrence University in Appleton, Wisconsin. She now writes full time for over a dozen feminist magazines and has contributed to a number of books, including ghostwriting on the topic of abortion for Gloria Feldt, president of Planned Parenthood. She doesn't hide her head in books however; Jennifer has been featured at feminist conferences sponsored by the United Nations and *Ms.* magazine and in the documentary film *Righteous Babes* (a title she well deserves). To learn more about this feminist, author, and political activist, visit http://www.soapboxinc.com/bio_jennifer.html or watch her contribute to the political roundtable on the weekly Oxygen Network TV show "She Span."

d.f. One of the things I asked Amy (your coauthor) about was your dedication at the beginning of *Manifesta* to all the women who say, "I'm not a feminist, but . . ." I was wondering if you could comment from your perspective about this dedication.

j.b. Writing that dedication was a breakthrough moment for us. We knew that we Bridget Jones types had not completely dropped the ball politically. We thought that our generation actually synthesized the messages from feminism and in some ways have been living these messages more honestly than our idealistic mothers did. We wanted it to be really clear that *Manifesta* isn't one of those books that will say, "This is to make you realize that you *are* a feminist." Instead, we're saying that where we are all starting from right now is *not* complete and total ignorance about feminism. So our book is dedicated to all the women who say I am or am not a feminist but what does this mean? I'm a feminist but can I wear a thong? I'm a feminist but do I have be like the women I learned about in my feminist theory class?

d.f. One of the major themes in Chick Lit seems to be the differences between our generation and that of our mothers. In *Manifesta* you talk about how we are not our mothers and the generational gap that women are facing today. Care to comment?

j.b. With my actual mom, I would say I have experienced this problem in wondering, If I don't replicate her life, then am I somehow undermining the value of her life? The first time I had a relationship with a woman, my mother read my choice as a real judgment of her, heterosexuality, and her marriage to my dad. In some ways, breaking free from what your mom did is really a slap in the face, because our mothers don't have a lot of public affirmation of how they lived their lives. It's weird growing up and thinking, god I never would have contemplated getting married at twenty-one and having three kids right away, and I never would have felt like it was OK to be Mrs. David Baumgardner. But then again, I was raised by my mother to think this way. My mother was my primary influence about feminist issues, so I try to point this out to her as I make different choices. I am not rejecting her but learning to make my own decisions based on how she raised me.

d.f. In your story at the beginning of *Manifesta*, you ask the question, Why suffer in the name of feminism? You say when you and Amy wrote this book you did all kinds of fun things together, all while critiquing patriarchy. This makes me think about Chick Lit novels that are hilarious and fun, but at the same time about women getting respect and finding their life calling and someone to love. I was wondering if you could talk a little bit about your thoughts on this topic.

j.b. My question about "why suffer" was me rejecting a real message from older feminists to younger feminists. There was a sense that we were doing something wrong by doing fun things. We weren't on the barricades. We weren't shunning beautiful shoes. We were instead getting bikini waxes. Women will never really be liberated if we still believe that girls aren't allowed to go shopping, that we're the only ones who need to fix all the world's problems. It's very important for women to feel like they have a right to fun and for feminists to feel that fun is a part of feminism.

Having a writing partner for *Manifesta* helped make it a fun experience because then I had a girlfriend with whom to share things. The whole experience was very Chick Lit. Initially, when Amy and I were floundering with how we were going to write the book, we did all these things that lessened the stress—we went shopping and traveled to Cuba. Before the book we were already close friends, but then we became like sisters. This bond was the cushion that let us do the hard work of the book. To come together is this intimate bond you forge with your girlfriends, and you do it through these practices that aren't hyper-intellectual. But you *can* be hyper-intellectual when you're shoe shopping. I think Amy and I end up talking about some of the most important things when we were just walking to get a milkshake together.

d.f. One of the strongest themes in Chick Lit revolves around characters' experience in the workplace. The typical fantasy is somehow finding a way to get out of the workplace altogether and be your own boss and freelancer. What's your thought on the workplace today and women's desire to "get out"?

j.b. I feel like women are opting out of the workplace, and men would like to opt out because going to work sometimes feels like you're climbing into a cage. You are constantly supporting people—your children, your partner, your co-worker; you're disappointing everyone, and no one is happy because you're leaving a little too early for your boss or a little too late for your kids. A lot of very normal things that make life fun, like shopping, end up going by the wayside. You live a very deprived life in order to have both home and a family. There just aren't enough hours in a day, and you feel constantly like you're living behind the 8-ball. So I think that the cage is something any sane person would want to escape. I think work is a frontier that both women and men are going to have to take on.

d.f. Changing the topic a bit, would you mind talking about whether you have any religious background and where you are with religion and spirituality in your life?

j.b. I'm from North Dakota, and everyone there is Lutheran; I was raised Lutheran and I was baptized and confirmed. From the time I was little, though, there was a lot of questioning going on in my family about religion. I would question the church, like if God created the world then who created God, and no one had adequate answers for me. I had a lot of issues with things I thought the church was taking positions on that didn't seem very Christian things to do. I was very influenced by Christ's life at a young age because Christ seemed like the kind of guy you would want to hang out with and have as your ally. My pastors, on the other hand, did not seem like allies. So I developed this anti-Lutheran, pro-Christ sentiment that I still feel. In my life today, I've tried to go to church at Christmas, and I want to feel again that thing I felt a couple of times at church: goosebumps or something. I haven't felt goosebumps about church or God probably in a long time. But I still relate to Christ a lot as an activist—as a model for activism. I don't feel like the church or Christianity excludes me—I don't feel like it's fundamentally oppressive at all. So I believe in God and Christ, but I have total space for Judaism, Buddhism, and other religions, too. Religion doesn't threaten me, and I sense my place in it.

d.f. Would you tell readers a little bit about your new book *Grassroots*?

j.b. It's sort of like *Manifesta* part two, in that *Manifesta* ended with a call to activism and tried to define it a little bit—that it's not just something for crazy people who live in trees for a year. Amy and I do a lot of activism in so many ways, like buying a Hillary Clinton T-shirt in the Marc Jacobs store or talking openly about my STD or Amy's abortion. I think we both wanted to point out those types of things we do in the context of activism and explain how activism has a lot of entry points. *Grassroots* is really saying: "Look, you want to change something? You actually can." It's about using your power to find out the truth about something, to have an investment in your community and change something that you think is wrong. You need to do more than just sit in a bar and complain about things. Our message is that anything is figure-out-able just by making a few phone calls that then lead you somewhere else. We want people to know that anyone can create their own avenues into activism. We tell the stories of how a lot of regular women are making their own roads into doing something.

d.f. The way you chose your examples of activism sounds like my reason for writing about Bridget Jones and not Mother

Teresa—trying to understand what it means to grow spiritually when you're not a nun or Gandhi.

j.b. Bridget Jones has had way more effect on my life, and
I don't think there are many people who could be or would
want to be Mother Teresa, although what she did was amazing. Bridget Jones seems more real, and I feel like it is very
important for us to be honest about life. If we could only find
a way to not get overwhelmed about things but instead say,
"I'm a feminist but these are the things that are still in process," then we will be doing each other a service. I'm glad
that you talk about *Sex and the City* in your book. My friend
Elizabeth Wurtzel (author of *Bitch: In Praise of Difficult Wom-
en,* among other books), who I think is a real Chick Lit sort
of girl, commented in a talk recently about the foursome:
"Why are they so sane? Why are none of them in therapy or
on Prozac?" She answered that it was because they had community and weren't trying to live in this ideal "I'm a good feminist" world; they were living in their own world and making
tons of mistakes and having lots of heartbreak, but they had
each other, and they could process it over lunch every week
and they did. They were sane because of that. And they were
very resilient. I think the Chick Lit message is honest about
our flaws and our reliance on each other—it's about the
strength of having sisterhood—a more honest sisterhood than
generations past perhaps. And we are the ones creating it ourselves. We need to own this and make it visible.

Notes

Introduction

The quote from Jessica Reaves about hiding her copy of *Bridget* comes from her article titled "I'm a Feminist—and I Love 'Bridget Jones's Diary,'" *Time*.com, Apr. 13, 2001, http://www.time.com/time/sampler/article/0,8599,106224,00.html.

For articles that consider the relationship between feminism and Bridget Jones as a character, see Janelle Brown's "Is *Time* Brain-Dead?" from *Salon*.com, June 28, 1998, http://www.salon.com/media/1998/06/25media.html, and also Erica Jong's "Ally McBeal and *Time Magazine* Can't Keep the Good Women Down," that ran in the July 13, 1998, edition of the *New York Observer* and is reprinted on Jong's Web site, http://www.ericajong.com/nyobserver980713.htm. Both articles critique the antifeminist portrayal of characters like Ally McBeal and Bridget Jones by *Time*'s journalist Ginia Bellafante in June of 1998.

Bridget's attribution of weight gain to fictional baby "growing at monstrous and unnatural rate" is from Helen Fielding's *Bridget Jones's Diary* (New York: Penguin Books, 1996), 101. (Note: from here on out I refer to *Bridget Jones's Diary* as simply *The Diary*.)

The Heather Cabot quote about "Chick Lit" as the booming genre of literature written for women in their twenties and thirties was from her article, "Chick Lit: Genre Aimed at Young Women Fueling Publishing Industry," for ABC News, Mar. 30, 2004, http://abcnews.go.com/sections/wnt/Entertainment/chicklit030830.html. For more information on Chick Lit as a genre, see www.chicklit.com, which offers FAQ, articles, interviews, forums, and more.

For an informative article discussing how recent interest in Chick Lit from the Religion Books publishing industry has been dubbed by *Publisher's Weekly* as "Bridget Jones Goes to Church," see Deirdre Donahue's "Publishers Put Their Faith In Churchified Chick Lit," from *USA Today,* Oct. 30, 2003, http://www.usatoday.com/life/books/news/2003–10–29-church-lit_x.htm.

If you are wondering about the texts mentioned of "a more typical spiritual persuasion" like that of Teresa of Avila (a Spanish, Christian mystic from the sixteenth century), read a selection from *The Interior Castle,* trans. Allison Peers (New York: Doubleday, 1989), in addition to *Bhagavad-Gita: The Song of God,* trans. Swami Prabhavananda and Christopher Isherwood (New York: Signet Classic, 2002). The Bhagavad-Gita is the sacred text of Hinduism.

My comments about, "discovering the messier side of the divine: a god/dess that feels, cares, yearns, grieves, and who knows when life calls for laughter," have been influenced by many feminist theologians; perhaps most important was Carol P. Christ in *She Who Changes: Re-Imagining the Divine in the World* (New York: Palgrave MacMillan, 2003) and Grace Jantzen in *Becoming Divine: Toward a Feminist Philosophy of Religion* (Indiana: Indiana University Press, 1999).

The information on Britney Spears and Madonna claiming to be Kabbalists in the Jewish mystic fashion comes from an article by Debra Nussbaum Cohen, "A Surge in Popularity in Jewish Mysticism," printed in the *New York Times,* Dec. 13, 2003, A15.

If you are interested in Jewish mysticism beyond Britney and Madonna, a good introduction to Kabbalah is David A. Cooper's *God Is a Verb: Kabbalah and the Practice of Mystical Judaism* (New York: Riverhead Books, 1997).

Chapter One: The Confessions of a (Neurotic) Diary-Keeper

The excerpts from Kate Reddy's "Must Remember" lists, including "see brill new film Magic Tiger, Puffing Dragon?" and "get Jesus an exercise ball," as well as "My mother saying my name, Kissing a child's cold cheeks," are found in Allison Pearson's *I Don't Know How She Does It* (New York: Anchor Books, 2002), 85 and 225.

I say that it is *rare* that feminine language is used to talk about the divine, but one major exception to this rule is found in Hebrew scripture, in the Book of Wisdom, where the pronoun used for Wisdom (the Holy Spirit, or Sophia in Greek) is "she." I like Wisdom 7:22 in particular: "For Wisdom, the artificer of all taught me. For in HER is a spirit, intelligent, holy, unique,/ Manifold, subtle, agile, clear, unstained, certain, not baneful, loving the good, keen, unhampered, beneficent, kindly,/ Firm, secure, tranquil, all-powerful, all-seeing,/And pervading all spirits, though they be intelligent, pure, and very subtle." Not bad at all! Feminist theologian Elizabeth Johnson has used Wisdom-Sophia as a way of re-imagining the Christian Trinity in feminine language in her book *She Who Is: The Mystery of God in Feminist Theological Discourse* (New York: Crossroad/Herder & Herder, 1993).

The inspiring words of YHWH: "I will greatly increase your pains in childbearing; with pain you will give birth to children. Your desire will be for your husband and he will rule over you" are from Genesis 3:16. I refer to the God of Judaism as YHWH throughout this book, which most people pronounce as "Yahweh." YHWH is the second name given to Moses by God in Exodus. For more information on the etymology and naming of

God within the Jewish tradition, see "Exploring the Word of God," at http://www.wcg.org/lit/bible/law/namegod.htm.

If you are interested in Hildegard of Bingen, Christian mystic and visionary extraordinaire from the twelfth century, read her *Scivias,* trans. Mother Columba Hart and Jane Bishop (New York: Paulist Press, 1990). Also *Women Christian Mystics Speak to Our Times* by David Perrin (Wisconsin: Sheed & Ward, 2001) is a good introduction to a number of other medieval Christian mystics (including Julian of Norwich, Catherine of Siena and, of course, Hildegard).

A good article about how contemporary scholars are working to retrieve ancient goddess culture is Merlin Stone's "When God Was a Woman," in *WomanSpirit Rising: A Feminist Reader in Religion,* eds. Carol P. Christ and Judith Plaskow (San Francisco: HarperSanFrancisco, 1992), 120–130. Also for information on Hindu goddesses see David Kinsley's *Hindu Goddesses: Visions of the Divine Feminine in the Hindu Religious Tradition* (Berkeley: University of California Press, 1988).

Carol Christ's call for a "new literature for women" and the quote that "stories reveal the powers that provide orientation in people's lives" is from *Diving Deep and Surfacing: Women Writers on Spiritual Quest* (Beacon Press: Boston, 1980), 1–12.

Bridget's comment: "Wish had not been born but immaculately burst into being in similar, though not identical, manner to Jesus, then would not have had to have birthday" is taken from *The Diary,* 68, and her miracle vision that "sex prove[s] indeed to be the best form of exercise" is also from *The Diary,* 52.

The quotes about how "What is common to all [sacred] stories is not their genre but their function . . ." and "fiction, poetry and other literary forms are key sources for discovering the shape of women's spiritual quest," are also taken from Carol Christ's *Diving Deep and Surfacing,* 4 and 12.

"The telling" and "the hearing" and their role in claiming a text as sacred is discussed throughout Christ's chapter,

"Women's Stories, Women's Quest," in *Diving Deep and Surfacing,* 1–12.

Alex Kuczynski, writer for the *New York Times,* has been quoted rather often now for his scathing judgment of Bridget as being quite the self-obsessive, indulgent Chick. For more information, see Martha Bagnall's review of *The Diary* in the Winter 1998, Vol. 1, No. 4, issue of *The Yale Review of Books,* http://www.yale.edu/yrb/winter98/review04.htm.

If you'd like to delve into the "Dark Night of the Soul" with St. John of the Cross himself, check out his writings, in particular (v. shocking): *Dark Night of the Soul,* trans. Allison Peers (New York: Doubleday, 1990).

The Evelyn Underhill quotation, "the material for an intenser life" that "lies at our gates," is from her book *Practical Mysticism* (Columbus, Ohio: Ariel Press, 1986), 27–28.

Comments about Bridget from London's *Evening Standard* were taken from reviews of *Bridget Jones: The Edge of Reason* at http://www.penguinputnam.com/static/packages/us/bridgetjones/book.htm.

You can find a traditional definition of "eschatology" by A. T. Hanson in *The Encyclopedia of Christian Theology,* eds. Alan Richardson and John Bowden (London: SCM Press, 1989), 183–186.

For an example of how one feminist theologian has "read the silences" of women within sacred texts, in particular the Hebrew and Christian scriptures, see Elisabeth Schüssler Fiorenza's *In Memory of Her: A Feminist Theological Reconstruction of Christian Origins* (New York: Crossroad, 1998), 41.

Carol Christ's chapter, "Nothingness, Awakening, Insight, New Naming," from *Diving Deep and Surfacing,* 13–26, includes an insightful discussion about how women today need to learn how to "name" the spiritual and the sacred for ourselves.

The idea that we can and must all become "protagonists" in the unfolding of our spiritual journeys and growth is drawn from the work of *mujerista* theologian Ada María Isasi-Díaz in her book *Mujerista Theology* (Maryknoll, New York: Orbis Books, 2002), 128–147.

Chapter Two: Real Feminists Don't Wear Pink—or Do They?

Bridget's inner dialogue about nights "of drunken feminist ranting with Sharon and Jude" and Shazzer's depiction of men as "stupid, smug, arrogant, manipulative, self-indulgent bastards" are both taken from *The Diary,* 107–108.

The conversation about feminism between Bridget and her mum, where Bridget claims that "if you're a feminist, you shouldn't need a—[man]" and Mum calls feminism "silly" and claims that "Anyone with an ounce of sense knows we're the superior race," takes place in Fielding's *Bridget Jones: The Edge of Reason* (New York: Viking, 2000), 298–300. (Note: from here on, I refer to *Bridget Jones: The Edge of Reason* as simply *The Edge.*)

When I discuss how I don't quite feel like a feminist in manner of Betty Friedan (from the 1960s) or, more recently, Naomi Wolf (from the 1990s), I refer to what are now considered two classic texts in the feminist vein: Betty Friedan's *The Feminist Mystique* (New York: W. W. Norton, 2001) and Naomi Wolf's *The Beauty Myth: How Images of Beauty Are Used Against Women* (New York: Perennial, 2002). For another classic feminist text, see Simone de Beauvoir's *The Second Sex* (New York: Vintage, 1989).

For a text that provides "models of god" as mother, friend, and lover, see Sallie McFague's *Models of God: Theology for an Ecological, Nuclear Age* (Philadelphia: Fortress Press, 1989).

In discussing how our generation of women *does* have our own version of feminism, just one that's different from our mother's, I draw heavily from *Manifesta: Young Women, Feminism, and the Future* by Jennifer Baumgardner and Amy Richards (New York: Farrar, Straus, & Giroux, 2000). This is the same book dedicated to all of us who say "I'm *not* a feminist, but . . ." and others who say "I *am* a feminist, but . . ." I couldn't have written this section without the personal stories and ideas throughout *Manifesta*, and I highly recommend this book as a great read for any girl of our generation. Another interesting read about young women and feminism is the anthology *Listen Up: Voices from the Next Feminist Generation*, ed. Barbara Findlen (Emeryville, Calif.: Seal Press, 2001).

My comment about how women "organizing" can occur over lunch, goodies, or even a shopping trip was inspired by Jennifer Baumgardner's personal "Introduction" from *Manifesta*, xv–xxi.

Chapter Three: "Oh God, Why Am I So Unattractive?"
The conversation between Jude and Bridget where Jude, in response to Bridget's weight loss, comments that "Maybe you've lost it a bit quickly off your . . . face," and that ends with Bridget's thinking that "life's work has been a total mistake," takes place in *The Diary*, 91–93.

The scene where Bridget rationalizes a potentially tragic jail experience in Thailand into an excellent pound-losing, thigh-reducing affair takes place in *The Edge*, 246–259.

Please note! When I discuss the warning bells that go off with respect to my own and Bridget's obsessing about weight and how one of the empowering things about Bridget's obsessive calorie counting is that it helps us lighten up about and even laugh at our own struggles with our bodies, I am not in any way trying to minimize the tragedy that results when girls' and women's obsessions with weight lead to life-threatening battles with bulimia and anorexia. For resources in addition to Naomi Wolf's *The Beauty Myth* that explore our struggles with the body, see Susan Bordo's *Unbearable Weight: Feminism, Western Culture, and the Body* (Berkeley: University of California Press, 1995), Sharlene Hesse-Biber's *Am I Thin Enough Yet: The Cult of Thinness and the Commercialization of Identity* (New York: Oxford University Press, 1997), and Joan Brumberg's *Fasting Girls:*

The Emergence of Anorexia Nervosa as a Modern Disease (Cambridge, Mass.: Harvard University Press, 1988).

In researching how the Chick Lit genre has been criticized for its weight-obsessed, calorie-counting, bad-example-for-women heroines, I came across an interesting review by Teri McIntyre of *Good in Bed* (Jennifer Weiner). This article criticizes the negative role model that most Chick heroines provide us about body image and then holds up Cannie Shapiro as the lone positive example among the lot of Chick Lit. You can find McIntyre's review at http://www.empowerment4women.org/attitude/books/jenniferweiner_goodinbed.html.

The reference to Eve's naughty behavior that leads to the ejection of humanity from paradise (The Garden of Eden) can be found in the second creation story in Genesis 2:4–25.

The ideas about how experiencing their bodies and bodily changes passively, as *happening* to us in full view of everyone, are drawn from Valerie Saiving's discussion of women's development in her article, "The Human Situation: A Feminine View," from *WomanSpirit Rising,* 25–42.

The comment about how the Catholic Church goes so far as to forbid women to take precautions against getting pregnant, since they have to remain subject to "natural biological reproductive processes," comes from Elisabeth Schüssler Fiorenza's article, "Feminist Spirituality, Christian Identity, and Catholic Vision," in *WomanSpirit Rising,* 142.

Yes, it's true: Thomas Aquinas called women "misbegotten males" in his famous *Summa Theologica,* Vol. 1, Question 99, Part 2, when he answers the inquiry: "Whether, in the primitive state, women would have been born?" To see it for yourself, check out the online *Summa* at http://www.newadvent.org/summa/109902.htm.

Feminist theologian Sandra Schneiders describes what she calls "a paralysis of the religious imagination" in how we talk about and picture the divine in her book *Women and the Word:*

The Gender of God in the New Testament and the Spirituality of Women (New York: Paulist Press, 1986), 10.

Rita Gross's claim that the feminine personification of YHWH in the Jewish tradition is actually a *mitzvah,* or obligation, for the Jewish people is found in her article, "Female God Language in a Jewish Context" in *WomanSpirit Rising,* 167–173.

For a discussion of "God as Mother," see Sallie McFague's *Models of God,* 97–124; for "God as birth-giver to creation," see Dorothee Soelle's *To Work and to Love: A Theology of Creation* (Philadelphia: Fortress Press, 1984), 1–53; for God imagined through Wisdom-Sophia, see again Elizabeth Johnson's *She Who Is,* 86–99 and 124–149; and for a perspective of Jesus in feminine terms, see *She Who Is,* 150–169.

Carol Christ (the woman who knows all and to whom I keep referring) discusses "why women need the goddess" in her article, titled appropriately, "Why Women Need the Goddess: Phenomenological, Psychological, and Political Reflections," in *WomanSpirit Rising,* 273–287.

The idea that we are vulnerable, evolving, and loving and needing to receive love as embodied creatures so we need to imagine a divine who also encompasses these experiences and evolves with us is found throughout Carol Christ's *She Who Changes,* Dorothee Soelle's *To Work and to Love,* and in Grace Jantzen's *Becoming Divine.*

Chapter Four: "Forgive Us Our Trespasses!"

Daniel Cleaver's playful yet mocking comment to Bridget: "There goes your inner poise, my plumptious. Best place for it, I say," is found in *The Diary,* 96.

To brush up on your knowledge of the Seven Deadlies (i.e. Sins), they include the following: Envy, Gluttony, Lust, Greed, Sloth, Anger, and Pride. Oxford University Press has started a wonderful series on this subject, devoting one entire book (very attractively packaged I might add) on each of the Seven Deadly

Sins. If I were you, I'd peruse Simon Blackburn's *Lust: The Seven Deadly Sins* (New York: Oxford University Press), 204. Also you simply can't go wrong in digging up your old copy from college of *The Divine Comedy,* by Dante Alighieri, trans. C. H. Grandgent (New York: Random House, 1950), which deals with the Seven Deadlies as steps in the descent to hell (lovely).

For a traditional definition of venial sin, see Gerald O'Collins entry in *A New Dictionary of Christian Theology,* 595–596; for mortal sin see William Horden's entry in the same volume, 386. Thomas Aquinas's discussion of sin, both venial and cardinal from his *Summa Theologica,* is always a fun read (please insert sarcasm here). See again the online *Summa* on this topic at: http://www.newadvent.org/summa/208800.htm.

The idea that sin involves activity, be it intentional or unintentional, whose end result separates us from the divine and diverts us from our spiritual path, can be further explored in any of Dorothee Soelle's works, including *To Work and to Love: A Theology of Creation* and one of her most famous texts, *Suffering,* trans. Everett R. Kalin (Philadelphia: Fortress Press, 1984).

My comments about how in Judaism sin has traditionally been understood as an act of rebellion and an intentional betrayal of the Law, and therefore worthy of divine punishment, are drawn from Morris N. Kertzer's *What Is a Jew? A Guide to the Beliefs, Traditions, and Practices of Judaism That Answers Questions for Both Jew and Non-Jew,* revised by Lawrence A. Hoffman (New York: Simon & Schuster, 1996), 115–116.

See the following Web site: http://www.friesian.com/caste.htm, for an explanation of the Hindu caste system that also includes a discussion of Karma.

To explore further the idea that confession served a therapeutic or cathartic purpose that allowed early Christians to unburden their sinful thoughts, see Thomas Merton's *The Wisdom of the Desert* (New York: New Directions Publishing, 1988).

For a description of the Rosh Hashana and Yom Kippur, please see http://www.jewfaq.org/holiday4.htm and http://www.jewfaq.org/defs/days.htm. It also never hurts to consult *The Jewish Book of Why* by Alfred J. Kolatch (New York: Jonathan David Publishers, 1981) for your every Jewish question.

Valerie Saiving's ideas about transforming our under-standing of virtue from selflessness to divine engagement come from her article, "The Human Situation: A Feminine View," in *WomanSpirit Rising,* 36–41.

The critique of salvation as "denoting rescue" and the comments about flourishing as an alternative to salvation: "A movement or person 'in full-flourish' is a movement or person that is vibrant and creative, blossoming and developing and coming to fruition," come from Grace Jantzen's *Becoming Divine,* 160.

Chapter Five: "Am Irresistable Sex Goddess! Hurrah!"
The first section heading for Chapter Five—"Shag me! Shag me!"—is actually pulled from a longer statement by Bridget: "I felt like throwing myself after him shouting, 'Shag me! Shag me!'" from *The Diary,* 90. The "him" on this particular occasion refers to Daniel Cleaver.

I learned about Christian spin-off Chick Lit novels like Kristin Billerbeck's *What a Girl Wants: A Novel* (Nashville, Tenn.: W Publishing Group, 2004), which is not to be confused with the non-Christian spin-off *What a Girl Wants* by Liz Maverick of almost the same name, as well as that Christian-focused Chick Lit is being labeled "Bridget Jones goes to church," in an article by Deirdre Donahue, "Publishers Put Their Faith in Churchified 'Chick Lit,'" from *USA Today,* Oct. 30, 2003, http://www.usatoday.com/life/books/news/2003–10–29-church-lit_x.htm.

Christopher West's bad news about sex for Singleton folk that premarital sex equals selfish gratification, and the notion that "luckily," if we've already "blown it" and given up our virginity,

Jesus Christ will forgive us if we renounce our evil sinful ways, is taken from his book *The Good News About Sex & Marriage: Answers to Your Honest Questions About Catholic Teaching* (Ann Arbor, Mich.: Servant Publications, 2000), 65–71.

In addition to Marion Zimmer Bradley's fabulous novel *The Mists of Avalon* that tells of the ritual shagging elements of goddess culture, see Starhawk's article, "Witchcraft and Women's Culture," in *WomanSpirit Rising,* 258–268, for more on the Goddess in relation to the Horned God and springtime, ritual sex.

My comment about how, unless you are Smug Married you must guard your purity *at all costs,* comes from the seemingly endless Evangelical books out there today about how we all must preserve our purity, including the following favorites: Stephanie Moore's *Staying Pure* (Chicago: Moody Press, 2000) and Rebecca St. James's and Dale Reeves's *Wait for Me: The Beauty of Sexual Purity* (Nashville: Thomas Nelson, 1997).

For more information about the notion that a woman who does not remain a virgin is punishable by death in some religions (often called "honor killings"), see Hillary Mayell's article, "Thousands of Women Killed for Family Honor," in *National Geographic News,* Feb. 12, 2002, http://news.nationalgeographic. com/news/2002/02/0212_020212_honorkilling.html.

The ideas about marriage and virginity within Hinduism, Buddhism, and Jainism, as well as the erotic quality found within marriage in Islam and Orthodox Judaism, are drawn from Elizabeth Abbot's *A History of Celibacy: From Athena to Elizabeth I, Leonardo da Vinci, Florence Nightingale, Gandhi, and Cher* (New York: Scribner, 2000), 163–196.

My comments about how in the Muslim faith there are "ten parts" to desire, and women represent nine, can be further explored in Geraldine Brooks's *Nine Parts of Desire: The Hidden World of Islamic Women* (New York: Anchor Books, 1995).

The lovely concept that in having sex before we are married we are committing an act of adultery against God (!) is found throughout Joshua Harris's *I Kissed Dating Goodbye: A New Attitude Toward Romance and Relationships* (Sisters, Ore.: Multnomah Books, 1997).

The quote from Daphne Merkin that "If a man can't handle his urges, advises the Talmud, he should go to a neighboring town and seek relief," is taken from her article, "The Woman in the Balcony: On Rereading the Song of Songs," in *Out of the Garden: Women Writers on the Bible* (New York: Fawcett Columbine, 1994), 244. Jewish feminist Judith Plaskow discusses similar ideas about the concept of adultery and sex with regard to women in her book *Standing Against Sinai: Judaism from a Feminist Perspective* (New York: HarperSanFrancisco, 1990), 4.

Bridget's ruminations about "The New Celibacy" takes place in *The Edge,* 274–283. An interesting article about Born-again Virginity called "The New Virginity: Why More Teens Are Choosing Not to Have Sex" by Lorraine Ali and Julie Scelfo appeared in *Newsweek* (Dec. 9, 2002), 61.

The quote about Bridget Jones and the distinction she makes between sex and spirituality: "Look, am not supposed to be thinking about sex. Am spiritual," is from *The Edge,* 274.

In addition to perusing the Kama Sutra for another example of how the erotic seeps into spiritual tradition, read the poems of medieval Christian mystic Hadewijch of Antwerp in *Hadewijch: The Complete Works,* trans. Mother Columba Hart (New York: Paulist Press, 1980). For some more contemporary texts on this topic, there is a really interesting article on the spiritual side of sex by scholar James B. Nelson called, "Reuniting Sexuality with Spirituality" from *The Christian Century* (Feb. 25, 1987), 187–190; it also appears at the following link: http://www.religion-online.org/cgi-bin/relsearchd.dll/showarticle?item_id=114. Also take a look at Fran Ferder's and John Heagle's *Tender Fires: The Spiritual Promise of Sexuality* (New York: Crossroad, 2002).

I quote Elaine Pagels about authority from her interview in the February 2004 issue of *The Believer,* 81–82.

The ideas about how spiritual sex requires a community of two, as well as a certain degree of love, commitment, and affirmation of both parties, are discussed in more detail in another book I wrote with my friend Jason King (so I am shamelessly referencing myself here) called *Save the Date: A Spirituality of Dating, Love, Dinner, and the Divine* (New York: Crossroad, 2003), 103–125.

Chapter Six: "Up the Fireman's Pole"

My knowledge that Meg Cabot approaches the workplace with a "what goes around comes around" mentality in manner of Karma comes from my interview with her that can be read at the end of this very book!

Although I do make the claim that women have finally broken free of the double grip, defying both societal and religious patriarchy and pursuing our passions through the job market and public life, we must remember that in many Orthodox religions, especially in certain parts of the Muslim world, women are still basically not allowed out of the house. For a vivid account of the Muslim woman's experience, see Azir Nafisi's *Reading Lolita in Tehran: A Memoir in Books* (New York: Random House, 2003).

For an interesting article that discusses the rat race we experience in the workplace, see feminist Rita Gross's article, "What Went Wrong: Feminism and Freedom from the Prison of Gender Roles," from *CrossCurrents,* Vol. 53, No. 1 (Spring 2003), found online at: http://www.crosscurrents.org/Grossspring2003.htm.

If you would like to wallow in the abyss with French existentialist philosopher Albert Camus, then you should read his famous essay on Sisyphus in his book *The Myth of Sisyphus and Other Essays* (New York: Random House, 1955).

The discussion about work as a torture-like, treadmill experience is drawn from Dorothee Soelle's chapter on the subject called "Work and Alienation," from her book *To Work and to Love: A Theology of Creation,* 55–67. Soelle's claim that: "Good work releases the divine element in us," is also taken from *To Work and to Love,* 96. Finally, the ideas about work as requiring three "magical qualities," including self-expression, relationship, and connection to nature also come from Soelle's *To Work and to Love,* 83–113, since she is very prolific and all-knowing about the subject of work and spirituality.

For information about the life and writings of medieval mystic Catherine of Siena, who corresponded with the Pope (including Gregory XI) during her lifetime (quite a shocking accomplishment for a woman at the time), see *Catherine of Siena: The Dialogue,* trans. Suzanne Noffke (New York: Paulist Press, 1980).

Grace Jantzen has a wonderful discussion about the significance of women visionaries in her book *Power, Gender, and Christian Mysticism* (New York: Cambridge University Press, 1995).

I quote James Horne's ideas that a "person decides to undertake important projects or missions, or even their vocation in life, in the midst of the mystical process" and also that "mystical illumination" is a "central visionary experience . . . that results in the resolution of a personal or religious problem," from his book, *Mysticism and Vocation* (Ontario, Canada: Wilfred Laurier University Press, 1996), 9.

Grace Jantzen's claim that "Projections need to be those which embody our best and deepest aspirations, so we are drawn forward to realize them" and further discussion about projection is found in *Becoming Divine,* 90–92.

Chapter Seven: Bread and Wine Among Friends

The discussion about Paul, the early Christian community at Corinth, ritual invisibility, and spiritual homelessness is found in Peter Brown's *The Body and Society: Men, Women, and Sexual Renunciation in Early Christianity* (New York: Columbia University Press, 1988), 33–64.

I talk a lot about Evangelical Christianity and Orthodox Judaism emerging as almost fads among younger generations. A new 'zine just came out this year that targets the Evangelical youth world called *Relevant Magazine*. Check it out at www. relevantmagazine.com. The *Boston Globe Sunday Magazine* also did a really interesting article on the growing phenomenon among Evangelicals of the college age in an article called "God on the Quad," by reporter Neil Swidey on Nov. 30, 2003. You can check the article out online at: http://www.boston.com/news/globe/magazine/articles/2003/11/30/god_on_the_quad/. For a good book by a formerly cultural Jew turned Orthodox Jewish twenty-something, read Wendy Shalit's *A Return to Modesty: Discovering the Lost Virtue* (New York: Simon & Schuster, 1999).

For more information about the yearly ritual that honors Brigid, called the festival or feast of Imbolc, see the following Web sites: http://druidry.org/obod/deities/brigid.html, as well as http://druidry.org/obod/festivals/imbolc/index.html.

I briefly discuss the importance of ritual and how ritual is supposed to help us distinguish the sacred from the normalcy of life, that is, the sacred from the profane. Ritual, symbol, sacred space, and the concept of "spiritual performance" I have found to be fascinating topics in my study of spirituality and religion, and I highly suggest the following classic texts if you are interested in looking further into this topic: Mircea Eliade, *The Sacred and Profane: The Nature of Religion,* trans. Willard Trask, (Pennsylvania: Harvest Books, 1968); Mary Douglas, *Purity and Danger: An Analysis of Concepts of Pollution and Taboo* (Great Britain: Penguin Books, 1966); Peter Berger, *The Sacred Canopy: Elements of a Sociological Theory of Religion* (New York: Anchor Books, 1990); and Paul Ricoeur, *Figuring the Sacred: Religion, Narrative, and Imagination* (Philadelphia, Fortress Press, 1995).

I quote the idea that "We have to welcome mind, body, heart, and soul into the learning process" and discuss the notion of "spiritual leadership" from Judy Rogers's wonderful article,

"Preparing Spiritual Leaders: One Teacher Takes on the Challenge," from *About Campus,* Vol. 8, No. 5 (Nov.-Dec. 2003), 19–26.

Chapter Eight: "Have You Noticed Anything Odd About Your Mother?"

My discussion of the "Martyr Mum" and the following quotes about Martyr Moms as "passive-aggressive, making dinner for eight when they're exhausted, and then later hating you for it, essentially ceding their own lives in the thankless service of others" and women who wear "self-denial like a blue ribbon," are from Jennifer Baumgarnder's and Amy Richard's discussion of this subject in *Manifesta,* 211.

I quote Bridget's mummy as a good example of the Martyr Mum when she says guilt-inducing things like, "I'll be all right on my bloody own. I'll just clean the house like Germaine sodding Greer and the Invisible Woman," taken from *The Diary,* 42.

Character Kate Reddy's comment about her sister-in-law's husband: "Peter plays the valuable role in Cheryl's life of the Cross I have to Bear. Every martyr needs a Peter, who, given time, can be trained up to not recognize his own underpants," appears in Allison Pearson's *I Don't Know How She Does It,* 42.

The idea that the vast majority of women were once expected *not* to cultivate any life or autonomy of their own for the sake of serving husband and children *until recently,* may indeed be more prevalent today for many women in Western society. Yet even in the West, Ada María Isasi-Díaz discusses how Latina women as a group face great challenges against the machismo understanding of family within Latin culture in her chapter, "Elements of a Mujerista Anthropology," in *Mujerista Theology,* 128–147. In addition, the total sacrifice of self is still the norm in Muslim and Hindu society. For more information on the role of women in the family within Islam and Hinduism, check out the following resources: *Islam, Gender, and Social Change,* ed. John Esposito and Yvonne Hadid (New York: Oxford University Press,

1998) and Santana Flanigan's Web site, "Arranged Marriages, Matchmakers, and Dowries in India," which can be read online at: http://www.emory.edu/ENGLISH/Bahri/Arr.html.

For a definition and description of martyrdom as "witness" within Christianity, see W.H.C. Frend's entry, "Martyrs, Martyrdom, Martyrologies," in *A New Dictionary of Christianity,* 347–349.

Baumgarder's and Richard's comment that, "for mothers, the challenge is to realize that their daughters came of age in an entirely different era, one that makes their lives fundamentally different," is taken from *Manifesta,* 214.

The idea that Jewish identity is centered on the family, not only in terms of worship within the home and education of children into the faith but also that the survival and future of the Jewish people rests on one's children growing up, marrying another Jew, and having lots of offspring is an interesting issue within Judaism, especially since it is *through the mother* that the Jewish lineage is continued: "the faith of the mother determines the faith of the child." For more on the role of the woman in a Jewish family, see Carol Ochs's article, "Miriam's Way" (from which I take the above quote), in *CrossCurrents,* Vol. 45, No. 4 (Winter 95–96), 493–509. This article may also be found online at: http://www.crosscurrents.org/Miriamsway.htm.

The article where I read recently that people of all faiths, including Muslims, Christians, and Jews, were banding together (in admirable act of interfaith unity) to protest the impending horrors of gay marriage becoming legal in the United States (please note that I find it deplorable that this is a source of interfaith union), is found in the editorial section of *America: The National Catholic Weekly,* Vol. 190, No. 6 (Feb. 23, 2004), 4.

The *New York Sunday Times* (from the "Week in Review" section) on Mar. 28, 2004, includes an article titled, "The Power of Adult Clothes in a Youth-Obsessed Culture," by Ginia Bellafonte. Her article discusses the field of psychology's acknowledgment of the new "emerging adulthood" phase in human development. Though I must note that emerging adulthood according to psychology apparently only extends to age twenty-six, leaving out all the many Singletons still busy emerging as adults well into our thirties.

The discussion of personal identity as a kind of "apartment of the self," one that we can construct, deconstruct, and reconstruct, is drawn from Jewish feminist Laura Levitt's article, "Becoming an American Jewish Feminist" from *Horizons in Feminist Theology: Identity, Tradition, and Norms* (Minneapolis: Fortress Press, 1997), 154–164.

Chapter Nine: Tick-Tock Goes the Biological Clock

Magda's hilarious commentary while she is on the phone with Bridget when she asks her husband: "Has he done it in the bed? A wee or a poo? IS IT A WEE OR A POO?" is taken from *The Edge,* 171.

For a really interesting book about motherhood, our conception of what becoming a mother means (or is supposed to mean), and our sense that motherhood is still our destiny, check out Susan J. Douglas's and Meredith W. Michaels's *The Mommy Myth: The Idealization of Motherhood and How It Has Undermined Women* (New York: Free Press, 2004).

I comment in this chapter that historically, within most religions, the experience of motherhood has been viewed as *the pinnacle* of possible spiritual experiences for women. However, it is also important to remember that, at least with respect to today's world religious traditions, a woman's biological capacity for children has *also* historically provided one of the tallest obstacles between women and the divine, especially within the Catholic tradition (v. paradoxical: see chapter on body for more information about this).

To read Pope John Paul II's lovely treatise, *Mulieris Dignitatem,* that glorifies a woman's reproductive capacity in terms of giving her a special dignity and role in the Church, see the following Web site: www.wf-f.org/MulierDig.html#MDIntro (includes the document in full).

Again, with regard to the notion that within Judaism the role of the mother is prized, as the survival and perpetuation of Israel rests within the mother's womb, I will refer you back to Carol Och's article, "Miriam's Way," from *CrossCurrents*.

The idea that in the Muslim tradition a woman's primary function is to produce heirs, and women who bear sons are afforded more rights than those who do not (as men must have sons for their honor within Muslim society), comes from the scholarship of Liela Ahmed's *Women and Gender in Islam* (New Haven: Yale University Press, 1992), 20 and 28. See also Geraldine Brooks's *Nine Parts of Desire*, 66–69.

The complex identity struggle that some women face within traditional religion, leading a woman to fear she is *less* of a woman if she does not become a mother, is explored in its many dimensions in Anita Diamant's beautiful novel *The Red Tent* (New York: Picador USA, 1997).

My discussion of archaeological evidence of ancient goddesses represented in figurines of women idols with pregnant bellies, known as "Venus figures," as well as how ancient Paleolithic cultures usually traced their ancestry to a deified "Divine Ancestress," revering a female divine-mother figure as the ultimate creator similar to YHWH, is drawn from Merlin Stone's article, "When God Was a Woman," in *WomanSpirit Rising*, 124–127. For additional resources on the "Divine Ancestress" and ancient goddess culture that centers on women, motherhood, and fertility, see the following: Elaine's Pagel's article, "What Became of God the Mother: Conflicting Images of God in Early Christianity," also in *WomanSpirit Rising*, 107–119; all of Part One from the anthology, *Weaving the Visions: New Patterns in Feminist Spirituality*, ed. Carol P. Christ and Judith Plaskow (San Francisco: HarperSanFrancisco, 1989), 15–92; and Joyce Tyldesley's *Daugh-*

ters of Isis: Women of Ancient Egypt (London, England: Penguin Books, 1995).

I mention that in addition to the Chick Lit genre there exists what people are calling Mommy Lit. The most famous novel that so far falls under the heading Mommy Lit (though it also counts as Chick Lit) is Allison Pearson's *I Don't Know How She Does It,* but other titles include Jane Green's *Babyville* (New York: Broadway, 2003) and Adele Parks's *Larger Than Life* (New York: Downtown Press, 2003).

When I talk about the Great Goddess who also "gave birth" to understanding woman as Warrior, Wise Counselor, and so on, as is the case with the Goddess Sarasvati in India, as well as how in Celtic culture, it is the goddess *Brigid* who is considered the patron of language, I base this discussion again from Merlin Stone's article, "When God Was a Woman," from *Woman-Spirit Rising,* 120–130.

The Wicca tradition's interpretation of fertility over the course of a woman's life cycle in terms of the phases of the moon is further discussed in Starhawk's *The Spiral Dance: The Rebirth of the Ancient Religion of the Great Goddess* (New York: HarperCollins, 1989).

Chapter Ten: All Goddesses Have a Romantic Side (or Ten)
The Sunday Styles article I reference about the final episode of *Sex and the City* is, "Do We Need Men to Be Happy?" and it was published in the *New York Times* by Ginia Bellafante, Feb. 22, 2004, Section 9, 1. You can read it online at: http://www.nytimes.com/2004/02/22/fashion/22CARR.html?ex=1083643200&en=1a50d6f22ca06176&ei=5070.

I insinuate that people you wouldn't even imagine were worried about the outcome of the series *Sex and the City,* in light of a surprisingly favorable article by a Catholic priest, James Martin, who was sorry to see the series go and talks about his nostalgia in the following article: "Sex—and Reality—in the City," from

America: The National Catholic Weekly, Vol. 190, No. 5 (Feb. 16, 2004), which you can read online at: http://www. americamagazine.org/gettext.cfm?textID=3417&articletypeid= 37&issueID=472&search=1.

Bridget's description of the Zen-Flow-like state that has her "relaxing and going with the vibes" and allowing her to "live in the moment" takes place in *The Diary,* 83.

Ariana Ghasedi's and Andrew Cornell's complaints that characters like Bridget Jones are women who "feel worthless without male validation," among other ideas, can be found at http://www.zmag.org/ZMag/articles/feb01cornell.htm from Feb. 2001 for zmag.com, that, interestingly, happens to be a book review of *Manifesta* in which Ghasedi and Cornell criticize that authors Richards and Baumgardner are wrong in claiming that Bridget and Ally McBeal are feminist figures for a younger generation.

A good feminist book about the question of whether a woman needs or desires a man, how this affects a woman's identity (negatively), and what all this has to do with sex is Naomi Wolf's book *Promiscuities: The Secret Struggle for Womanhood* (New York: Ballantine Books, 1998).

For a very fascinating yet rather densely intellectual look at women, men, and the mirror issue, see postmodern feminist and psychoanalyst Luce Irigaray's *Speculum of the Other Woman* (that's right, you heard me correctly: speculum) trans. Gillian C. Gill (Ithaca, N.Y.: Cornell University Press, 1985).

All the references from Paul's letter to the Corinthians in the New Testament about men serving as the head for women within Christianity, and so on, are found grouped together in a document called "The Status of Women in the New Testament Epistles" at: http://www.religioustolerance.org/nfe_bibl.htm.

If you are interested in reading the myth of Narcissus and Echo, you can find it online at: http://www.loggia.com/myth/echo.html.

To learn more about the mystic's journey inward to the core of the self, in addition to reading the various texts I have suggested from medieval women mystics like Julian of Norwich, check out Evelyn Underhill's classic text called *Mysticism* (England: Oneworld Publications, 1999). A good anthology about mysticism is edited by Richard Woods, *Understanding Mysticism* (New York: Image Books, 1980).

When I discuss a Christian seeking intimacy with Christ, a Jew seeking Kabbalistic knowledge, and a Buddhist monk seeking a nirvana, I want to clarify that since Buddhism is not a theistic religion, a Buddhist monk seeking nirvana is seeking out the experience of nothingness rather than what most traditions refer to as the divine. I also want to note here that though many scholars of mysticism understand mystical experience as universally the same across all religions, there is debate within scholarly circles about whether or not the divine intimacy encountered on the mystical journey *is* really universal or not. Scholars like Grace Jantzen claim that the ethics and rituals of each religion inform both the mystical journey to God and its impact on the mystic's life, making the experience different in accord with each tradition, historical, political situation, and gender.

Christian mystic Bernard of Clairvaux ruminates on verses from *The Song of Songs* like, "He kisses me with the kisses of his mouth," in *Bernard of Clairvaux: Selected Works,* trans. G. R. Evans (New York: Paulist Press, 1988).

The following quote from Sufi poet Hafiz about the experience of loving God as if a game of tag, when in playing, God suddenly "Has kissed you and said/You're it/I mean, you're really IT!" comes from his poem, "You're It," in *The Gift,* trans. Daniel Ladinsky (New York: Penguin Compass, 1999), 30.

I quote "bitter and dark and desolate/Are Love's ways in the beginning of love," from Hadewijch of Antwerp's poem, "Becoming Love with Love," from *Hadewijch: The Complete Works,* 224.

The famous lines: "When love beckons to you, follow him"; "To know the pain of too much tenderness"; and "Give your hearts, but not into each other's keeping" come from the famous Jewish poet Kahlil Gibran's *The Prophet* (New York: Alfred A. Knopf, 1997), 11–16.

Chapter Eleven: "Human Beings Are Like Streams of Water"

Bridget's v. enlightened, v. funny conversation with Mark Darcy about self-help books as a new religion and where she observes that, "It's almost as if human beings are like streams of water so when an obstacle is put in their way, they bubble up and surge around it to find another path," is found in *The Edge,* 58–62.

The idea that what Bridget calls "spiritual epiphany" a Hindu might call unity with the "Universal Spirit," which for a Buddhist may involve seeking fusion with the "Pure Light of the Void," and for a Christian may mean entering into eternal marriage with the Godhead of the Trinity is drawn from Aldous Huxley's "Introduction" to *Bhagavad-Gita: The Song of God,* trans. Swami Prabhavananda and Christopher Isherwood (New York: Signet Classic, 2002), 11–22.

If you are interested in reading about St. Augustine's conversion from being a Manicheism to Christianity, see *The Confessions,* trans. R. S. Pine-Coffin (New York: Penguin Books, 1961).

For resources about mysticism understood as "spiritual epiphany," mystical experience as possibly universal core experience to all religions, and the idea, supported by some scholars, that the religious dimensions of spiritual epiphany are merely the "clothing" of the moment that needs to be "stripped away" to encounter the pure center within the experience (in addition to those that I suggest in Chapter Ten on this topic), see the anthology *Mysticism and Philosophical Analysis,* ed. Steven T. Katz (New York: Oxford University Press, 1978).

Sacred texts from Buddhism to read include the following: *The Dhammapada: The Sayings of the Buddha,* trans. John

Ross Carter and Mahinda Palihawadana (New York: Oxford University Press, 2000) and *Buddhist Wisdom: The Diamond Sutra and the Heart Sutra,* trans. Edward Conze (New York: Vintage Books, 2001). There are also some interesting feminist perspectives on Buddhism that tackle the issue of relinquishment of desire, the devaluation of the body, and so forth, found within this tradition, including the following anthology: *Buddhist Women on the Edge: Contemporary Perspectives from the Western Frontier,* ed. Marianne Dresser (Berkeley, Calif.: North Atlantic Books, 1996).

Bridget writes in her diary to "get money from somewhere. Maybe Buddha?" in *The Edge,* 278.

My discussion about William James's three categories of people: the Healthy-Minded, the Divided Selves, and the Sick Souls is from his famous *The Varieties of Religious Experience* (New York: Collier Books, [1902] 1961), 78–159.

Catherine Keller's description of humanity and the world in manner of a great "cosmic sponge," with metaphorical "water" that streams in and out of our porous lives and relationships— water that is, in fact, *grace*—is drawn from her book *Face of the Deep: A Theology of Becoming* (New York: Routledge, 2003), 81–82.

Epilogue

Ada María Isasi-Díaz's discussion about the role of the *fiesta* in Latina spirituality is found in her chapter "Elements of a Mujerista Anthropology," in *Mujerista Theology,* 130–131.

The Author

Donna Freitas is a professor of spirituality and religion at St. Michael's College in Colchester, Vermont, where she is known to wear stylish yet impractical shoes in all manner of weather. She received her Ph.D. from the Catholic University of America and her undergraduate degree in philosophy from Georgetown (Go Hoyas!). Donna is coauthor of *Save the Date: A Spirituality of Dating, Love, Dinner, and the Divine.* When she's not devouring Chick Lit novels and designer chocolates or hanging out with the people she loves, her research and speaking center on pop culture and women's spirituality. Donna lives with her husband in Burlington, Vermont. They are unSmug Marrieds.

Get to know Donna Freitas and join the discussion about Inner Poise at www.DonnaFreitas.com.